Bound by Conflict

D1462148

# Bound by Conflict
## Dilemmas of the Two Sudans

**FRANCIS M. DENG**
IN COLLABORATION WITH **DANIEL J. DENG**

**THE CENTER FOR INTERNATIONAL HUMANITARIAN COOPERATION**
AND **THE INSTITUTE OF INTERNATIONAL HUMANITARIAN AFFAIRS,**
**FORDHAM UNIVERSITY**
NEW YORK 2015

Library of Congress Control Number: 2015945495

Printed in the United States of America

17 16 15    5 4 3 2 1

First edition

CONTENTS

In 2010, Francis Deng wrote a brief but comprehensive study, *Sudan at the Brink: Self-determination and National Unity*, which outlined the past, present, and prospective future of conflict in the country, united or divided. A referendum was to be held in the South in January 2011 to determine whether the country would remain united or be partitioned by Southern independence. I provided a Foreword, which I was pleased to do, especially as I had known Francis since the early 1960s when I was in the Sudan as a young physician, and we later grew closer together and cooperated on a number of books and other activities. The book, published by Fordham University Press, as part of its International Humanitarian Series, was immediately translated into Arabic, German, and French and available in electronic form, in order that it have the most broad contribution on the rapidly evolving national debate.

The referendum in South Sudan was only a few months away. And yet, while anticipating that the South would predictably vote for independence, there were international apprehensions about Southern independence. Francis Deng himself entertained a faint hope that unity within the framework of a New Sudan of full equality, without discrimination on the base of race, ethnicity, religion, culture, or gender, might still be possible. I shared the delicate balance between his realistic assessment of the situation, which favored partition, and optimistic aspiration for unity.

In my Foreword, I wrote:

There is grave concern over partitioning the country and the repercussions not only for Sudan, but also the Continent of Africa as a whole, and by extension, the global community. Even in material terms, the international community has already invested billions in humanitarian assistance to Sudan, and the United Nations and the African Union maintain two major peacekeeping operations in the South and Darfur. Unless the Southern referendum and results are carefully and constructively managed, the international community could be confronted with yet another crisis with grave humanitarian and fiscal consequences.

I also commented on the role of Francis Deng specifically:

This book is a powerful statement by an individual who is deeply concerned about the plight of his people and the destiny of his country, a man who in many ways, symbolizes the lofty aspirations for unity, in which diversity is seen as a source of enrichment and not of destructive conflict, a unity of full equality among all its citizens.

I went on to acknowledge the fact that Sudan had not lived up to those aspirations:

Unfortunately, Sudan has so far failed to rise to this lofty vision. If the voters choose unity, it must be implemented in a far more equitable manner than in the past. If they opt for secession, then the process of partition must be as peaceful and harmonious as possible, with both North and South working to establish a framework for close association and cooperation, while leaving open the possibility for reunification, should the right conditions be created.

Francis Deng, in his Introduction, also wrote:

Whatever the decision of the South on the issue of unity and secession, the two parts of the county will remain in the same geographical proximity, will continue to interact, and, in varying ways, will become even more interdependent than they have been. All this means that there will undoubtedly be significant elements of unity beyond partition. Unity and partition represent degrees of relationship. The challenge for the North and the South is to work out the arrangements that will reconcile partition with ongoing challenges of unity.

My observations and those of Francis Deng were supported by many prominent personalities, including three Nobel Peace Laureates, leaders from Africa, the United Nations, and academia.

Tragically, the concerns that Francis Deng articulated in *Sudan at the Brink*, which were widely shared by the international community, are now being played out in proliferating conflicts within and between the Two Sudans. But Francis Deng, with his characteristic optimism, believes that there are always opportunities in crises and that both Sudan and South Sudan should see these interconnected crises as wake up calls for them to debate what went wrong and what they must do to correct it. *Bound by Conflict: Dilemmas of the Two Sudans* reflects the spirit of his long commitment to a Sudan united on the basis of full equality for all, with no discrimination on the basis of race, ethnicity, religion, culture, or gender. Even after the partition of the country, in accordance with the vote in the 2011 referendum that overwhelmingly chose secession, in light of the current conflicts within and between the two countries, the Two Sudans are still being called upon to pursue the ideals of a New Sudan. Achieving this goal would provide a basis, if not for full reunification, at least for some association that would foster peace, security, stability, and cooperation between them.

He sees the violence that broke out in December 2013, and soon escalated into a rebellion, as significantly rooted in the long North–South war in the Sudan. Government's recruitment of tribal militias to fight a proxy war against the rebel movement, massive supply of small arms to these militias, the conclusion of the Comprehensive Peace Agreement (CPA) as a result of international pressure, an agreement that was comprehensive only in the issues of North–South conflict that it covered, but by no means comprehensive to the country as a whole, the ambivalent, flawed, and in some cases antagonistic implementation of the CPA, unresolved conflicts in regions of the North bordering the South whose impact spills over the borders, differences over the sharing of the revenues from the oil produced in the South, and ongoing allegations of support for each other's rebels are among the contributing factors that keep the two countries still bound by conflict.

This means that for them to be bound together by peace, rather than by conflicts, they need to cooperate in resolving their internal conflicts to facilitate cordial bilateral relations, and prevent internal conflicts from spilling over their borders and impacting negatively on their bilateral relations. This is an obvious wisdom, which the parties in conflict are not likely to see or heed. They need international support, if only for face-saving reasons, to move in that direction.

Seen from this perspective, *Bound by Conflict* is a natural sequel to *Sudan at the Brink*. The two books are complementary. The future of the Sudan, South Sudan, and their prospective relations remain in a delicate balance between war and peace. What these two books are advocating is a win-win alternative to a zero-sum conflict that could become genocidal. As with his previous writings on the Sudan, Francis Deng's message in *Bound by Conflict* indicates an unfinished job of transforming the Sudan, starting with a credible implementation of the CPA. This book challenges the two independent countries, after the partition, to address their respective crises both internally and in their bilateral relations. In Francis Deng's view, it is by addressing the internal contradictions in both countries to consolidate peace and unity within each country that the Two Sudans can enjoy peaceful and cooperative relations between them. This is a message which should be taken seriously by all those concerned with the crisis in South Sudan and the connection to the Sudan.

Kevin M. Cahill, M.D
*University Professor and Director*
*The Institute of International Humanitarian Affairs*
*Fordham University*
*May 13, 2015*

## ACKNOWLEDGMENTS

Some of the materials in this book derive from reports prepared in projects on CPA implementation that were funded by the U.S. State Department and the U.S. Agency for International Development (USAID) between 2006 and 2007. I acknowledge their support with deep appreciation. I would also like to acknowledge the invaluable contribution of Ms. Vanessa Jimenez, who assisted me in my work on these projects. My son Daniel Jok has given me valuable support in preparing the book, as he has done on a number of other publications. I am deeply grateful to him and I acknowledge him as a collaborator. Winnie Kassa assisted with the preparation of the manuscript at various stages. My nephew Arob Bol Deng worked diligently on preparing the final copy-edited text. I am very grateful for my dear friend Kevin Cahill's championing of the book and his agreeing to write the Foreword. His son Brendan Cahill was instrumental in promoting the publication of the book in cooperation with Fordham University Press. The Provost of Fordham University, Stephen Freedman, Ph.D., and the Assistant Vice President and Chief of Staff, Ms. Ellen Fahey-Smith, saw the timely importance of the book, and once again Mr. Fredric Nachbaur and all at Fordham University Press have worked so hard to make sure this book was published so quickly and professionally.

While I acknowledge the support of institutions and individuals as noted above, the views expressed in this book are mine, and I am solely responsible for any errors of information and judgment and any other shortcomings of the book.

# Introduction

Sudan has been at war with itself since its independence on January 1, 1956. South Sudan became independent from Sudan on July 9, 2011. On December 15–16, 2013, South Sudan exploded in violence—initially within the presidential guards—that soon escalated into a civil war that increasingly assumed an ethnic dimension. Ironically, despite the sharp differences between the grievances that inspired the struggle of the South against the North and those that inspired the internal Southern conflict, there is a common thread between the two situations: the desire of ethnic and regional groups to be self-determining and self-governing in opposition to control by the perceived dominant ethnic groups that wield central national power and resources.

The vision of a New Sudan of full equality, without discrimination on the basis of race, ethnicity, religion, culture, or gender, was conceived, postulated, and championed by Dr. John Garang de Mabior, the leader of the Sudan People's Liberation Movement and Army (SPLM/A), who was tragically killed in a helicopter crash on July 30, 2005. This vision still applies to both countries, though in contrasting ways. Sudan was dominated by an Arab Islamic minority, which not only distorted its mixed African Arab identity, but imposed that distorted self-perception with an associated version of radical Islam to define a country of racial, ethnic, religious, and cultural diversity as Arab Islamic. South Sudan, a nation of over sixty-four ethnic groups, all African, with multiple belief systems including both traditional and imported

Christianity and Islam, cannot be defined by one group. If anything, each group in South Sudan considers itself at least equal, if not superior, to all other groups, and certainly subordinate to none. This poses severe challenges for leadership, but makes the country inherently democratic compared to the Old Sudan.

The smooth, peaceful, credible conduct of the unity-separation referendum in south Sudan provided for in the Comprehensive Peace Agreement (CPA) was a remarkable demonstration of the yearning for freedom. The result of the vote in favor of independence, over 98 percent, was stunning but not surprising. It was an outstanding rejection of what Southerners, including their brethren in the Ngok Dinka area of Abyei, had endured for more than fifty years during the so-called independence of the Sudan. It was also evidence of the resilience of the human spirit and the determination to struggle for freedom, however long it might take.

The Southern struggle for freedom has, however, left a legacy for Sudan as a whole. Self-determination and independence have been the core elements of the Southern struggle, and a mix of idealism and pragmatism has allowed the leadership of the SPLM/A to challenge the country with the vision of a New Sudan of full equality and nondiscrimination. This lofty vision inspired regional movements in the North to either join the South in the struggle, which the southern neighbors, the Nuba and the Ingessana, did in the 1980s, or wage their own autonomous struggles, which was the case with the Beja in the east and the Darfurians in the west.

However, the elusiveness of the New Sudan vision, the failure to achieve it by military means, and strong pressure for peace from the international community made the SPLM/A accept a negotiated settlement with the government of Sudan (GoS). But the crisis continues in the North. Indeed, while Southerners jubilated over their spectacular vote in favor of independence, and declared their independence on July 9, 2011, people in Abyei and parts of the North were still wailing over their dead and dying. It is now widely accepted that the proliferating regional conflicts in Sudan are rooted in a pervasive national identity crisis. The crisis initially dichotomized the country into the dominant Arab Islamic North and the grossly disadvantaged African South, where the population predominantly adheres to traditional belief systems but has increasingly converted to Christianity and, to a lesser degree, Islam. This crisis is still threatening to tear North Sudan apart along the same identity lines. Some believe what is happening in South Sudan is comparable to what Sudan has been experiencing. But there is a difference.

The crisis of national identity in Sudan is reflected in two distortions. The first is that the dominant minority at the center, though visibly an African Arab hybrid, perceives itself as monolithically Arab, with Islam and Arab culture as complementary ingredients. The second is that this already distorted self-perception is projected as a national identity framework, which becomes inherently discriminatory of non-Arabs and non-Muslims. This has been at the core of the conflicts that have devastated the country since independence.

The longest and most devastating conflict was the North-South war that raged intermittently for half a century from 1955 to 2005. The first phase of the war, from 1955 to 1972, was secessionist, but was resolved through a compromise agreement that granted the South regional autonomy. The unilateral abrogation of that agreement ten years later triggered the second war, from 1983 to 2005. The objective of that war was not secession but a new, united Sudan of full equality, without discrimination on the basis of race, ethnicity, religion, culture, or gender. The war was precariously resolved eventually by the CPA of 2005, which resulted in the independence of the South. The conflict situation in South Sudan is somewhat different in that while leaders from the sixty-four ethnic groups vie for power, a struggle that involves interethnic competition, no one group can claim dominance over the country or claim to identify the country exclusively with itself. The challenge is therefore the equitable management of pluralism among groups that can legitimately claim equality.

Although the CPA brought relative peace between Sudan and South Sudan, there are still areas of conflict between them that need to be addressed. Among these is the conflict over Abyei, at the North-South border, home to the Ngok Dinka, who are racially, ethnically, culturally, and geographically Southern, but who since colonial days have been administered in the North. The people of Abyei joined their kith and kin in the South in the first war, and were given the right by the 1972 Addis Ababa peace agreement to decide whether to remain in the North or join the South. That provision of the agreement was never honored by the government, which triggered a local rebellion in Abyei that eventually fueled the wider Southern rebellion and the return to war in 1983, in which the sons and daughters of Abyei played a major role and sacrificed a great deal.

The Abyei Protocol of the CPA granted the people of Abyei the same right granted in the 1972 agreement: to decide through a referendum, to be conducted simultaneously with the Southern referendum, whether to join the South or remain in the North. However, the implementation of the protocol has been obstructed by Sudan's ruling National Congress Party (NCP). The Missiriya were used by successive governments in the North as militias to fight the rebels in the South, but turned their guns against the civilian population, especially in the Ngok Dinka area. Since the independence of South Sudan, the Missiriya, in cooperation with the Sudan Armed Forces (SAF), and allied militias, have been openly threatening war, and have repeatedly invaded the area, in opposition to the implementation of the Abyei Protocol, a stance supported, if not instigated, by the NCP. Although the parties have agreed not to go to war over Abyei, a local rebellion in the area could win wider Southern support that could trigger a conflict against the will of the ruling parties in the South and the North, as indeed happened in 1982, which contributed to the resumption of the North-South war in 1983. It is now widely recognized that Abyei is a potential flashpoint that could plunge the North and the South back into war. Indeed, as the South was casting votes in the independence referendum, Abyei was once again attacked, and people died on both sides, but South Sudan chose not to jeopardize its independence by going to war with the North.

Also potentially destabilizing to the relations between Sudan and South Sudan is the situation in the border states of Southern Kordofan and Blue Nile. Their populations are predominantly African, and, though mostly Muslim, are also religiously mixed with Christians and traditional believers. Elements from these regions joined the SPLM/A in the war against the government in the mid-1980s. A special protocol in the CPA entitled their people to a "popular consultation" to ascertain their views on their status under the agreement. What this meant, and what was expected to be the outcome of the popular consultation, was never made clear, and it has remained vague, subject to controversial interpretation.

Almost as devastating as the North-South conflict is the atrocious situation in Darfur that has ravaged the region since 2003. The conflict has pitted the government and its Arab militias, known as the Janjaweed, against the rebel movements composed of mostly non-Arab tribes. While competition over scarce resources is a major factor in the conflict, inequitable management of racial and ethnic diversity among peoples who should otherwise be united by their shared Islamic faith is also a decisive factor. The Darfur Peace Agreement (DPA) of 2006 was stillborn and never stood any chance of credible implementation. The Beja of eastern Sudan, who are Muslim but non-Arab, also engaged in a low-level rebellion. The objectives of this conflict were similar to those of the other regional rebellions, but they were milder in intensity. The conflict was halted by the 2006 Eastern Sudan Peace Agreement (ESPA) brokered by Eritrea, but its implementation remains uncertain, and peace in the region is precarious.

The people of Nubia, which borders Egypt to the far north and is the most exposed to the Arab Islamic assimilation, though not engaged in armed rebellion, are also challenging the status quo and have revived their pride in their Nubian heritage. As one of their leaders jokingly intimated to me, they would rather pursue their cause with intelligence than with guns. They have, however, increasingly been associating themselves with the SPLM/A in the search for a common approach to the national identity question.

What do all these regional conflicts have in common? One word that is often used to explain the root cause of these proliferating regional conflicts is *marginalization*, the denial by the Arab center of the political, economic, social, and cultural rights of the populations in these peripheries. Although the non-Arab populations in the marginalized regions of the North have been assimilated into the Arab Islamic mold, the struggle of the South and the SPLM/A vision of a New Sudan have inspired them to rediscover themselves and demand equal recognition for their shared African identity.

After Southern independence, the marginalized non-Arab regions of the North have continued to struggle for a New Sudan of equality, and they look to the South for support. Should the South offer such support, the NCP would encourage and manipulate ethnic tensions in the South to generate proxy conflicts that would destabilize the country. Whether South Sudan has been supporting SPLM/A and whether Sudan has retaliated to destabilize the South are allegations being made and denied by both sides, and they have not been verified beyond doubt.

While the CPA apparently addressed the concerns of the South, it did not resolve Sudan's national identity crisis comprehensively. Instead of being a tool for democratic transformation, it became a weapon for the containment and entrenchment of the North-South divide even before the referendum, the vote for Southern independence, and the actual independence of South Sudan. This means that the marginalized non-Arab regions of the North remain victims of a distorted and discriminating national identity framework. Even with the independence of the South, the North continues to be challenged by the crisis of identity. As noted earlier, while the South jubilantly celebrated its independence, regions of the North continued to wail from the scourges of war.

A comprehensive resolution to the crisis of national identity in both Sudan and South Sudan would require a framework that guarantees full equality to all the peoples of the two countries. It must also ensure genuine autonomy for all the identity groups and regions, allowing them to be self-governing and to have an equitable share in the government of national unity, with a fair distribution of power, wealth, services, and development opportunities. Whether the arrangement is called decentralization, autonomy, regionalism, federalism, or confederation is less important than the substantive distribution of powers and resources at various levels of the government structure.

Since the outbreak of interethnic violence in Juba on December 15–16, 2013, and the rebellion that followed, it is particularly essential that the leaders of the North and the South do their utmost to prevent ethnic violence that could result in mass atrocities. Particularly vulnerable are the internally displaced persons (IDPs), who, though now being protected in UN compounds, fear facing potentially hostile groups outside, whether this is merely perceived or is factually grounded. It is also crucial that the international community be vigilant in ensuring the protection of all the populations, should their own states manifestly fail to protect them, as reflected in the Responsibility to Protect (R2P or R to P) principle, which was the outcome of the 2005 Summit of Heads of State and Government. This concept is now widely recognized as being founded on the concept of Sovereignty as Responsibility that colleagues and I developed in the Africa Project of the Brookings Institution toward the end of the Cold War era.

All this requires a leadership that can exercise the concept of responsibility and create the needed national framework of unity and full equality. There is no doubt that a leadership that is factional and espouses a divisive agenda for the nation cannot pursue this lofty vision with credibility. What both Sudan and South Sudan need is a leadership that rises above factionalism to represent all the peoples of their respective countries without discrimination. This is the vision that the Sudanese people, united or divided along the North-South line, must pursue, and it is a vision that calls for support from the international community. It is also a vision that would lay the foundation for a reunification of the two Sudans, not necessarily on the conventional understanding of one united country, but on a new association between the two independent, neighboring countries, building on mutual economic interests and common historical and cultural heritage.

The challenge for South Sudan is to find an opportunity in the current crisis by posing some tough questions about how the country descended to this point. What did we do that we should not have done, or did not do that we should have done? What can we do to correct what went wrong? What do we need constitutionally, institutionally, organizationally, and operationally to guarantee that this painful experience ends and does not repeat itself? I hope this book will contribute constructively to the debate and help move toward the desired objective of genuine peace, unity, reconciliation, stability, and nation building.

This book aims to elucidate several themes in order to substantiate the interconnectedness of the conflict situations in the two Sudans.

First, the conflicts within these countries spill over their borders and generate tensions and conflicts between them, especially as each of them accuses the other of supporting their rebel groups.

Second, the ambivalent implementation of the CPA, with many unresolved issues—in particular, the status of Abyei and the situation in the two border states of Southern Kordofan and Blue Nile—indicates an unfinished move toward a truly comprehensive and sustainable peace.

Third, internal displacement, which became a correlative of refugee status since the partition of the country, also indicates the persistence of the crisis, connected to the root causes of conflict in both countries.

Fourth, the North-South war, which resulted in the recruitment, training, arming, and deployment of tribal or ethnic militias by the government in Khartoum to fight proxy wars for them in the South, has left a legacy of militarization of the society, which provided ready manpower for the armed rebellion of the SPLM in Opposition in December 2013.

Fifth, these developments have had a paradoxical impact on the profile of South Sudan, entailing a dramatic shift from being favored as the youngest member of the United Nations with a legitimate demand for self-determination to being seen as proving right the prophets of doom, who predicted that South Sudan would be a failed state that would endanger the peace and security not only of its citizens and the region, but also of the international community.

Sixth, this has drawn the attention of the subregional, regional, and international organizations, both in efforts to end the conflict and to scrutinize and hold accountable those considered responsible for perpetrating the violence, gross violations of human rights, and atrocity crimes. This is reflected in the recent decision of the UN Security Council that adopted a framework for a sanctions regime against South Sudan, thereby subjecting it to the same treatment that Sudan has been subjected to for decades.

These themes confirm the thesis that unless the two countries resolve their internal conflicts, their bilateral relations will remain tense and conflictual. What is needed is a comprehensive resolution of the internal and interstate conflicts. This can be brought about by addressing the shared challenges of managing diversities constructively toward inclusivity, equality, and nondiscrimination on all grounds, including race, ethnicity, religion, culture, and gender. If this is accomplished, it should lay a foundation for some form of association between the two independent states.

# Chapter One: Overview of the Crisis

## A Dream Turned Nightmare, and Worse

For decades, the South Sudanese liberation struggle was the beacon of hope for those who wanted Sudan to be transformed into a country of inclusivity, equality, and nondiscrimination, a country whose citizens would enjoy the dignity of belonging without discrimination on the basis of race, ethnicity, religion, culture, or gender. Now, as South Sudanese wake up, they discover that their dream has not only turned into a nightmare, but, worse, that their country is falling apart in intensive ethnic violence. The violence erupted within the presidential guard on December 15, 2013, and soon escalated into a rebellion that quickly spread like wildfire to several states. Adversaries had used the possibility of such a rebellion as a reason for opposing the independence of South Sudan, but, though predictable on the basis of objective ethnic and historical factors, the warning signals were not heeded, and no preventive measures were taken.

During the six-year interim period and the two years of independence, South Sudan seemed to prove the prophecies of doom wrong, almost to the point of complacency. While intertribal violence, human rights violations, and rampant violent crimes continued to manifest themselves as remnants of the long North-South Sudan civil war that had militarized the society and created a culture of violence, South Sudan's independence still seemed a promising venture, especially given the amount of goodwill the new country enjoyed in the international community. And yet, in my public statements and private conversations with the leadership of South Sudan, I continuously argued that we must prove the prophets of doom wrong every day and avoid becoming complacent.

Relations between Sudan and South Sudan remained a challenge and a threat to sustainable peace, security, and stability across the two Sudans' borders. The conflicts in the two countries remained intertwined due to the rebellions within Sudan, especially among those in Southern Kordofan and Blue Nile who had been allies of South Sudan, as well as various militias in South Sudan that Khartoum had recruited, trained, armed, and unleashed to wage a proxy war against the SPLM/A. The uneasy relations between the two countries became a cause of great concern to the international community.

The international community was also becoming increasingly critical of the government of South Sudan (GoSS) on issues of financial mismanagement, especially with reports of rampant corruption, and it was demanding reform and accountability. President Salva Kiir, in response to these allegations and to the open criticism of his leadership by his vice president and the secretary-general of his party, the SPLM, suspended two leading ministers on allegations of corruption and dismissed his vice president, Dr. Riek Machar; the secretary-general of his ruling party, Pagan Amum; and leading members of his government. He eventually dissolved his whole cabinet, and, after a period of uncertainty, appointed a new one that included members of Sudan's ruling party, the NCP of the Islamic Front. Khartoum rejoiced, and Sudan and South Sudan, especially their respective presidents, became closer, a development that was welcomed by the international community but proved divisive within the SPLM/A.

The dismissed veterans of the SPLM/A armed struggle, including Vice President Riek Machar, initially seemed to take the president's decision in good grace. But, in retrospect, that might have been the calm before the storm that exploded on December 15, 2013, the immediate causes of which remain controversial. The government's version is that it was an attempted coup, while the opposition argues that it was the result of interethnic differences and misunderstandings among members of the presidential guard that the government is projecting as an abortive coup to incriminate its opponents. Some of the Nuer leaders argue that it was a retaliation against an attempted purge of Nuer elements of the Presidential Guard.

Given the known tensions within the SPLM/A and the armed rebellion of Dr. Riek Machar that soon followed the violence of December 15–16 aimed at overthrowing the government, the debate that raged over whether what happened was an attempted coup or not seemed superfluous, as the objective of each was the same: unlawful change of the government. A different perspective is raised by the so-called detainees who did not believe that there was a coup attempt and that they were certainly not involved in any such attempt. This is reflected in the reports of my meetings with them, in Juba, with the four detained there, and in Nairobi where those remaining were transferred. The international community viewed the crisis as essentially political, and felt it should be addressed as such.

The targeted killings of members of the Nuer community on December 15–16 were profoundly shocking to the nation. Even the Dinka, whose members had allegedly committed the atrocities, were outraged. President Salva Kiir himself declared that those who were targeting the Nuer in his name were not for him, but against him, and ordered them to stop. That did not, however, stop the escalation of the violence along ethnic lines or eliminate the perception that the government, led by a Dinka, pitted the Dinka against the Nuer.

The interethnic violence that soon engulfed the nation, spreading from Juba to the states of Jonglei, Upper Nile, and Unity, became notorious to the world. It is, however, important to put this national catastrophe in perspective. Such an exercise can be approached by taking several aspects into account.

First, South Sudanese societies, in particular the Nilotics, have long been documented by anthropologists as exceedingly ethnocentric, autonomous, and egalitarian. They are intensely resistant to authoritarianism. These are characteristics of an indigenously democratic society, but they make the country difficult to govern in a modern state-centric system.

Second, their culture has been presented as structurally acephalous and stateless, characterized by a segmentary lineage system in which those who identify as one group unite against an external adversary, but once that external adversary is removed, become divided among themselves, down to the level of clans, families, and even individuals. It is what the famous British anthropologist Professor Edward Evans-Pritchard, when describing Nuer society, called "balanced opposition" resulting in "ordered anarchy," a system of governance devoid of centralized coercive power of the state.

Third, despite this internal orientation, groups enter into alliances with external interest groups for support against their immediate adversaries, who are closer to them than the external allies. This explains the use of South Sudanese militias by the Sudanese government against their own South Sudanese freedom fighters.

Fourth, traditionally, power has been structured around two major role divisions: Chiefs and elders are peacemakers, while the youth, organized into warrior age sets, find their identity and dignity in warring, often using the slightest provocation to go to war, against the wise counsel of their elders. These young warriors are motivated in significant part by the desire to impress their female counterparts, who are metaphorically their future wives and who sing songs of praise for their husbands-to-be in their capacity as warriors. It is from this perspective that the role of females can be transformed to promote peace instead of values of masculine violence.

The end result is a paradoxical system that both emphasizes peace, unity, harmony, and reconciliation and is warlike, pragmatically soliciting external support for divisive, anticommunal advantages in conflict situations. This complex conflict situation calls for a multifaceted approach to both internal and external conflicts within and between Sudan and South Sudan.

First, unless there is internal peace in Sudan and South Sudan, there can be no sustainable peace between the two countries. The reverse is also true: Without peace between the two countries, there can be no peace within either of them.

Second, the basis for peace within and between the two Sudans has to be a genuine system of decentralization or devolution of power that gives all identity groups, however small, the right to govern themselves, be the primary beneficiaries of the resources in their areas, and have an equitable share in the national power and wealth distribution. As noted earlier, whether such a system is called autonomy, federation, or confederation is not as important as the manner in which powers and resources are distributed. The real objective must be that all groups, whether they identify themselves ethnically or geographically, large or small, must feel in charge of their own affairs and have an equitable share of national power and wealth.

Third, Sudan and South Sudan have a mutual interest in the way the two countries manage their diversities to achieve internal unity, peace, harmony, and a common sense of identity and national purpose. When I was undersecretary-general and adviser to the UN secretary-general on the prevention of genocide, I visited Juba and gave a public lecture organized by the Human Rights Office of the UN Mission in South Sudan (UNMISS) on July 29, 2011, only twenty days after independence, on the theme of diversity and nation building. A summary of the lecture posted by UNMISS stated, "Dr. Deng has urged his compatriots to recognize and manage their diversity so as to build a strong and vibrant state." The summary went on to say, "Diversity is a phenomenon which successful nations have endeavored to manage so as to promote a sense of common belonging, dignity and respect. . . . The independence of South Sudan has been brought about by the lack of effective diversity management mechanisms by successive Governments in the North. . . . If the new nation of South Sudan wants to build a strong and inclusive state, it should not repeat the same mistakes. . . . South Sudan struggled for so long on the basis of the principles of democracy and good governance." The summary added, "Deng calls on the leaders to respect and build on these ideals."

Fourth, the militarized youth must be given a positive interest in peace through training and employment, away from violence as the source of identity and dignity. In Nilotic traditional society, a boy had to reach a certain age of maturity, not much different from the required international standard of eighteen, before he could be initiated into a warrior age group. Unfortunately, this tradition seems to be abused by armed groups, encouraging boys who are eager to become men and warriors to be initiated at a much younger age than is traditionally required and be recruited into their militias or armed forces as what is now known as child soldiers. This has given South Sudan a bad image in the international community, which is particularly unfortunate as it also violates indigenous cultural values related to the rules of war.

Fifth, women, and especially girls, have an important role to play in fostering peace. If young men display their valor in war to impress females, who sing for them in praise, then by condemning war as a show of manhood and instead praising peace, they might influence men toward the value of peace.

Building on these interconnected conflicts and challenges, the two countries need to put their houses in order internally and thereby improve their bilateral relations. Reforming their governance systems toward the vision of a New Sudan of full equality, without discrimination on the basis of race, ethnicity, religion, culture, or gender, would make the systems in the two countries more compatible than they have been and therefore enhance cooperation between the two independent states.

## Tracing the Roots of the Crisis

It has always been my deeply rooted belief that every crisis also presents opportunities. This belief is an act of faith that is in part reflective of my optimistic disposition, which is in turn based on my conviction that optimism is a motivation for positive action, while pessimism leads to a dead end. But optimism should not be blind faith, or it, too, would lead to disappointment. There must be a basis for believing that what is optimistically desired is indeed achievable. This calls for analyzing the root causes of problems in order to develop strategic ways of addressing them. So, where does one begin the search for opportunities in the current crisis in South Sudan?

### Background to the Crisis

A brief look at South Sudan's recent history is a worthwhile starting point for understanding the current crisis. In a broad sense, the present situation should be seen in the context of South Sudan's history as an area of the Sudan that was neglected during colonial rule, and exploded in conflict with the central government in the North at the dawn of independence. That conflict lasted intermittently for half a century.

While the British administrators maintained law and order with very limited presence on the ground at the lower level, and effectively used indirect rule through traditional leaders, there were hardly any structures of governance in most rural areas of South Sudan, and no social services, except for rudimentary education and health care provided by the Christian missionaries as by-products of their main preoccupation, which was to recruit converts for their churches.

The situation was also characterized by ethnic diversity and the propensity toward violence among the warrior herding tribes, where cattle rustling, conflict over grazing lands and sources of water, and competing territorial claims often generated intercommunal violence. For these reasons, as well as an inadequate capacity for preventative governance, those who were opposed to the independence of South Sudan argued that it would be a failed state. They argued that once the uniting factor of the war with the North was removed, South Sudan would be torn apart by intertribal warfare. In many ways, the war itself prepared the ground for this prediction of doom, as tribal militias were recruited and supported by Khartoum to fight the Southern rebels by proxy.

With independence, President Salva Kiir promoted national unity, peace, and reconciliation by granting amnesty to the militias, most of whom were from the Nuer ethnic group, and incorporating them into the national army, the Sudan People's Liberation Army (SPLA). Former militias, mostly Nuer, composed an estimated 75 percent of the army. But they were not fully integrated and remained under their former commanders. This is why it was so easy for the former vice president, Dr. Riek Machar, to rally support within a short period of announcing his rebellion, following the eruption of violence among the presidential guards on December 15, 2013.

In terms of the immediate cause, the manner in which Vice President Riek Machar and Pagan Amum, the secretary-general of the SPLM, publicly criticized the president for alleged failed leadership, and the president's reaction—dismissing Riek Machar, Pagan Amum, and key ministers of his cabinet—should have been perceived as elements of an early warning. The crisis was compounded when the president then decided to dismiss his whole cabinet and reappoint a new one that included former members of the NCP of President Omar al-Bashir and excluded central figures in the leadership of the ruling SPLM.

These changes, which removed personalities that Khartoum considered hardliners against them, brought the leadership of the two countries, Sudan and South Sudan, closer, much to the satisfaction of the international community, which wanted relations between the two countries to improve. Little did they know, however, that the positive development of relations between the two countries was at the cost of internal cohesion and unity of purpose within the ruling party in South Sudan. The eruption of violence on December 15, 2013, was not predicted with any precision, but in hindsight, it should have been predictable in some form, and measures could have been taken to prevent it.

## Developments on the Ground

During this critical period, I visited the country on two occasions. My first visit was in the aftermath of President Kiir's dismissal of leading members of his government in rapid succession. The first to go were Deng Alor, minister of cabinet affairs, and Kosti Manibe, minister of finance, for authorizing payment for security installations in government buildings that was considered excessive in the amount paid and irregular in the procedures followed. These dismissals were strongly criticized by both Vice President Riek Machar and SPLM secretary-general Pagan Amum. President Kiir also dismissed the elected governor of Unity State, Taban Deng Gai, for which Vice President Riek Machar also criticized him. This was followed by the dismissal of Riek Machar and Pagan Amum, which was in turn followed by the dissolution of the entire cabinet.

After a period of suspense, during which the government was run by undersecretaries of the ministries, with oversight by the secretary-general of the government, the president formed a downsized cabinet. As noted, this excluded a number of senior ministers from the SPLM and included several South Sudanese former members of Sudan's ruling NCP. The political climate was reaching a boiling point, with open contestations for the presidency within the party leadership, including by Riek Machar and Pagan Amum. Tensions were ripe in the air and many, including prominent personalities, voiced their fears that the country might explode in violence. When I asked repeatedly what could be done to prevent that, I got no positive response. This clearly indicated that the leaders involved did not have a clear understanding of what was wrong and what could be done to correct it. Nevertheless, despite widespread dissatisfaction with the state of affairs, the dissident members of the SPLM, including Riek Machar himself, ostensibly ruled out the use of violence and committed themselves publicly to pursuing their cause through the political process.

During my first visit, I had the opportunity to meet with President Kiir, who explained to me in considerable detail the reasoning behind his decisions. He appeared very much at ease and satisfied with the decisions he had made. In particular, he said something I had already anticipated in my discussion of the situation with concerned persons abroad. He said he had come to the conclusion that his tolerant and conciliatory style of leadership was being misconstrued as weakness, and that he had to strike back to prove otherwise. I told him that I had myself given that explanation, but that I had also said in my discussions of the situation that if I had the opportunity to advise him, I would say that while his actions were understandable, in view of the way his vice president and SPLM secretary-general had behaved toward him, he should not allow that to change his character and the values for which he was known as a man of peace, unity, and reconciliation. I told him that he was what our people call a man with a "cool heart," which is an important attribute for leadership. The president nodded with apparent appreciation, and even said that he would reach out to "them," meaning his adversaries.

In my subsequent meetings with Riek Machar, Pagan Amum, and other former members of the cabinet, I found their attitude remarkably magnanimous, relatively understanding of the president's actions from his perspective and decidedly opposed to any violent reaction, but determined to push for political reform and their bid for the presidency. I left feeling encouraged that our leadership had reached a reassuring level of political maturity. And that was indeed what I expressed in my discussions of the situation within the United Nations and in the think tanks in the United States.

## Briefing the Ambassadors

My second visit to Juba was after the December 15–16 eruption of violence and the ensuing rebellion led by Riek Machar. The visit was part of the South Sudanese ambassadors meeting called by the government to brief them on the situation. The briefing was conducted by several ministers and focused on reaffirming that what happened was an attempted coup by Riek Machar and his followers, that it was not a Dinka-Nuer ethnic conflict, and that those responsible, some of whom were being detained, would be charged and tried for treason. A number of ministers elaborated on the impact of the conflict on the country from the perspectives of their ministries. The ministers were indignant that the world did not share the view of the government that there had been an attempted coup.

The briefings by the president and the successor of Riek Machar as vice president, James Wani Igga, chronicled the political tensions and conflicts within the ruling party that culminated in the eruption of violence on December 15 and 16, and the declaration of the rebellion by Riek Machar aimed at overthrowing a democratically elected government. The president and vice president shared the general disappointment that the international community did not believe the government's assertion that what happened was a coup attempt.

Nevertheless, I found the holistic approach of the president and the vice president, which traced the root cause of the crisis to a political confrontation within the leadership that ultimately erupted in the December 15 violence, quite convincing. I even raised the issue at the highest level of the judicial hierarchy: "Given the political conflicts within the party that exploded in the 15th December violence, and the declaration of the rebellion aimed at overthrowing the democratically elected government, does it really make a difference whether or not there was an attempted coup?" After making it clear that he would not express a political opinion, the answer from a leading judge was, "This is what the English call splitting hairs."

Whether we call it a failed coup attempt or a rebellion aimed at overthrowing an elected government, the normative principles involved are the same. The critical issue is whether the alleged coup attempt and the ensuing rebellion have a cause that should be addressed in order to achieve peace, unity, and reconciliation. My position is that people do not take up arms to kill and risk being killed without some cause that needs to be addressed. Suppressing violence with violence may be justified in some cases, but in the end, it is not the solution. We now know that beyond the quest for power, the rebels claim to have an agenda for reform, which should be addressed in the interest of peace and reconciliation.

The argument that the conflict was not ethnic and that there were Nuer and Dinka on both sides, while correct, underestimated the impact of the initial targeting of Nuers in the atrocities committed in Juba following the outbreak of violence on December 15 and 16. The speed with which Riek Machar mobilized the Nuer to his rebellion is a manifestation of the desire to avenge the targeted killings in Juba. Nevertheless, Riek Machar justifies his rebellion not as a cause of the Nuer, but as a national quest for the reform of the ruling party and the system of governance. This sounds reminiscent of the SPLM/A argument that their struggle was not to address a "Southern Problem," but a national problem of the Sudan. According to Riek, this is a cause shared by the eleven leaders who were arrested and detained following the December 15–16 violence.

## Meeting the Detainees

In my meeting with the president, I raised the issue of Riek Machar co-opting the detainees and argued that the fact that they were not being heard gave Riek Machar's claim some advantage. Although the minister of justice had said that in order to visit the detainees, a written request, stating the reasons for the intended visit, must be submitted to the committee investigating their alleged crimes—a procedure that discouraged potential visitors—I told the president that I wished to visit the detainees to hear their point of view and report back to him. He immediately approved my visit and instructed the minister of national security to arrange it. Seven of the detainees had just been released and were at the airport, about to be flown to Nairobi under the protection of the government of Kenya. I caught up with them at the airport to greet them, and I hoped to meet with them in Nairobi on my way back to the United States. I then went to meet with the remaining four detainees at the security headquarters.

I found the physical conditions of their detention quite comfortable and their spirit relatively positive. We had a very open, uninhibited discussion, during which they denied any involvement in a coup attempt and denounced Riek Machar's resort to violence, but maintained their original demand for a reform of the party and the system of governance in the country. The position of seven released detainees in Nairobi, who were given very comfortable accommodation by the government of Kenya, and whom I met on my way back to the United States, was basically the same as that held by their colleagues who were still in detention in Juba.

On my first meeting with the detainees in Juba, I wrote the following to the president:

At your kind permission, I visited, on January 29th, the four remaining detainees who are accused of having participated in the attempted coup of 15th December 2013. These are Pagan Amum, Oyai Deng Ajak, Majak d'Agot, and Ezekiel Gatkuoth. We met in the reception room of the national security headquarters.

The detainees were clearly pleased to see me and we immediately engaged in substantive discussion of the situation. I informed them that I had expressed my desire to visit them and that the President had spontaneously responded positively. Pagan Amum, who spoke the most, reflected their position. Denying that they were engaged in the coup attempt of the 15th December that was followed by the current rebellion led by Riek Machar, Pagan emphasized the extent to which the country has been torn apart by the ensuing violence. He argued that only the President could now rally national sentiment towards peace, unity and reconciliation. He referred in particular to the ethnic dimension of the violence, which is spreading across the country. He said that unless this is stopped, the country risks being Balkanized.

Most of those who spoke after him reaffirmed and added to what Pagan had said. Majak d'Agot, arguing that he did not think there was a case against them, said he would not even bother to have a lawyer and that if taken to court, he would defend himself. Oyai Deng Ajak said that he did not think that the problem was with the President himself, but rather with some members of his Government. In this connection, I told them that the level of anger among the public was extremely high and that there is a general sentiment demanding accountability for what has befallen the country. This outcry focuses on Riek Machar, especially as he had once before triggered similar violence through his 1991 coup attempt. Had he maintained his earlier rejection of violence and persistently called on people to refrain from violence, he would have maintained a higher moral ground. Instead, only two days after denying a coup attempt, he declared a rebellion aimed at overthrowing a democratically elected president.

Ezekiel Gatkuoth said that instead of reliving 1991, we should focus on ending the current violence. He said that the country is being fragmented on an ethnic basis, pointing out that there were no Nuer among the security forces around the detainees, nor are there Nuer on the streets of Juba, as most of them are staying in the UN compound. And in the areas where the Nuer are the dominant group, there are also no Dinka, except in the UN compound.

Overall, they lamented very much the violence that has engulfed the country, stressing that no one can accept what is happening. They said that they did not agree with Riek Machar in making their release a condition for the ceasefire and that for however long they might be detained, they strongly support the need for immediate cessation of hostilities. I explained to them that the President has strongly objected to anyone being killed in his name. He has consistently called for peace, unity and reconciliation for the country, and to move the country forward in the constructive process of socio-economic development and nation building. The President has also spoken of the need for immediate cessation of hostilities, provision of humanitarian assistance, release of detainees in accordance with the law, and pursuing negotiations to address the political crisis in the country and to facilitate overall reform of the national governance system.

In my concluding comments, I again expressed my deep appreciation for the President's allowing me to visit them and that he could have denied the visit on the grounds that the detainees were suspects who should not receive such a favor. They agreed and also expressed sincere appreciation for my having been allowed to visit them.

On my meeting with the detainees in Nairobi, I reported to the president the following:

Following my meeting with the detainees in Juba, which you kindly approved, I decided on my way back to the United States to arrange a meeting with the detainees who had been released to the care and protection of the Government of Kenya. I had, of course, seen them off at the airport in Juba, but they were nicely surprised and warmly receptive to my meeting with them in Nairobi. They are in very highly secure and comfortable accommodation.

Their perspectives were largely similar to those of the detainees in Juba about which I prepared a report for you, which I left with Cecilia (your assistant) to give you. They were, of course, interested in getting a briefing from me about the discussions in Juba, some of which they had followed on television. I told them that I found the briefings very helpful in that they gave our Ambassadors information that would help them in promoting the position of the Government abroad. I explained to them that there were three principal themes in the briefings we received. One spotlighted the events of 15th and 16th December as the core of the coup and related it to the eruption of violence in other areas, which made the coup seem well planned and coordinated. The other was a legal analysis by the Minister of Justice, which saw the coup attempt as treason, with all its other dimensions. The third, which was reflected by both the Vice President and yourself, elaborated on the incidents and events leading to and culminating in the 15th and 16th explosion. I said I found this the most helpful insofar as it made political developments, the violence of 15th and 16th December and the declaration by Riek Machar that he was leading a rebellion aimed at overthrowing the regime part of a process and not an incident.

Although they agreed that the conflict is not ethnic, they believe that escalation of the conflict was triggered with the targeting of different groups, which has given it an ethnic dimension. I pointed out that the President has consistently condemned ethnic targeting and did not want anyone killed in his name.

Like their colleagues in the Juba detention, they focused on the urgent need to end violence, to restore peace and unity, and to embark on a national reconciliation process with socio-economic development.

Both Deng Alor and Gier Chuang shared the positive exchanges they had with you and seemed to reflect a more optimistic view of eventually overcoming the problems and restoring peace, unity and reconciliation in the country, but all this they believe is premised on a sincere discussion of the differences that have caused these cleavages.

I am now back in New York and have started mapping out key circles to reach and share our perspectives with the objective of promoting cooperation with the United Nations. I am beginning with the P5 members of the Security Council, but hope to broaden the scope throughout the organization. Ambassador Akec and I are also in contact to prepare for the High Level Delegation that will be coming to Washington and New York to join our efforts in both contexts.

Once again, permit me to express my appreciation for the briefing and consultation meeting of Ambassadors, for seeing me amidst your heavy schedule, and for giving me permission to meet with the detainees, which has now enhanced my understanding of the situation. I feel better equipped to promote and defend the position of the Government than could have been the case before my return to Juba.

What I found to be critically important about my discussions with the detainees was that they confirmed what I had suspected and had shared with the president: that they were co-opted by the rebel leader, Riek Machar, and probably misrepresented as sharing his rebellion, especially as their voices were not being heard. My discussions with them made it clear that while they shared serious concerns with the rebel leader, and supported the call for reforms within the party and in the running of the country, they strongly opposed his use of violence as a means to the end they advocated. In that sense, the detainees could be potential allies in the quest for peace and reconciliation.

## The Tensions between the Government and UNMISS

A conspicuous aspect of the crisis in South Sudan was the rift between the country and the United Nations. This was most dramatically manifested by the public demonstrations against UNMISS and the special representative of the secretary-general, Hilde Johnson. Ms. Johnson and her UN colleagues felt particularly threatened by the political climate. When I went to meet Ms. Johnson, as I usually did when in Juba, I found her not in her office in the UN compound, or in her representational home, but in the UNMISS military barricade, in very modest, almost demeaning accommodations, considering the impressive residence that had been her official home. I was deeply touched by her condition and I felt sure that the authorities were not aware of what was happening to her.

Rather than enjoy the leisurely lunch to which Ms. Johnson had invited me, I rushed back to brief the foreign minister, Dr. Barnaba Marial Benjamin, who was about to leave for Addis Ababa. As I had predicted, the minister was totally unaware of Ms. Johnson's situation. Before going to the airport, he went to brief the president about the situation. The president, too, was surprised by what he heard, and he instructed the minister to make a statement affirming the country's commitment to protecting the special representative of the UN secretary-general and the UN personnel and reaffirming South Sudan's partnership with the United Nations. The foreign minister made a statement to that effect. Dr. John Yoh, the minister of education, who had been South Sudan's head of office in South Africa and later ambassador to Turkey, also supported our position with the president and in the cabinet. The president met with Hilde Johnson the next day and made a statement along the lines of the statement of the foreign minister. I also spoke to the press, radio, and television, recalling the strong support South Sudan had received from the United Nations and the international community in its march toward independence and during the post-independence reconstruction and the development of the country.

There was a national outcry when, because he had armed guards with him, the minister of information was denied entry into the UNMISS compound that accommodated internally displaced persons who sought protection from the violence. The refusal to allow him into the compound was seen as an insult to the dignity and sovereignty of the country. In my statements, I argued that while the reaction of the minister and the public was understandable, we should also try to understand the point of view of UNMISS, and I cited my own experience as representative of the secretary-general on internally displaced persons. I said that not only would I not allow armed guards into the IDP camps, I would not even allow government officials to enter the camps with me. After all, these were people fleeing threats from the government, and there was no way they would feel secure discussing their situation in the presence of a government representative.

To be sure, I had already heard many complaints against UNMISS on the grounds that the status of forces agreement (SOFA) was being abused by UN personnel. And, of course, UNMISS was also alleging violations of SOFA. The position of the government of South Sudan was presented to me in detail by the National Aliens Committee, which was comprised of leading officials of strategic ministries, mostly at the level of undersecretaries and director-generals. I shared their concerns with the special representative of the secretary-general, Hilde Johnson, who admitted that she had not heard of the committee, acknowledged that about 60 percent of the complaints were familiar to her, and agreed to my proposal that she should meet with the committee. The meeting was to be convened and chaired by the undersecretary of the Ministry of Foreign Affairs and International Cooperation, who was in New York at the time fixed for the meeting. As a result, the meeting was postponed and never took place.

Despite the statements by the minister of foreign affairs and the president and my own efforts to reaffirm a positive relationship with the United Nations, public demonstrations persisted against the UN, in particular against UNMISS, and Hilde Johnson personally, which some hardline voices in the government tended to encourage. This created a very unfortunate situation in which a country that had enjoyed so much goodwill and support from the international community began to be seen in a contrastingly negative light. Of course, we in South Sudan's Mission to the UN worked hard to counter this negative development in a constructive engagement with the secretariat, the Security Council, and key partners among the Permanent Missions.

Ironically, my own statement to the Security Council in which I attributed the anti-UN demonstrations to public frustration, trauma, and anger was misconstrued in the social media as supporting the UN against my country with allegations that my use of the word trauma meant that I was accusing the people of being mad. Statements by the presidential spokesperson accused me of not representing South Sudan. The issue was even taken to the cabinet for discussion, and it was only through the intervention of the minister of foreign affairs and the minister in the presidency, supported by other ministers, and the release of my statement to the cabinet that the crisis was averted and the relevant spokesman reprimanded. I myself was on the verge of resigning had the issue not been appropriately addressed, which I made known in a letter to the president.

In retrospect, as someone who witnessed developments from the standpoint of both the UN and South Sudan, I believe the roots of the crisis lay in the fact that there was a gap between the ambitious plans of the United Nations to assist South Sudan through UNMISS and the actual delivery on the ground, which was impeded by the inadequacy of resources. The contributing factor was the gap in communication at all levels between UNMISS and the national authorities.

As the crisis intensified into a civil war, which increasingly assumed an ethnic dimension, two developments proved to be of critical significance. One was that the United Nations, for the first time ever, opened its mission's compounds to those who were fleeing from the imminent threat of death throughout the areas of conflict, most of whom were from the Nuer community. Although a tragic incident happened in Bor, where Dinka youth broke into the UNMISS compound and killed an estimated thirty to fifty IDPs in the UN protection site, without that UN protection, so many more people would have been killed.

The second development, which also proved pivotal to protecting the lives of civilians, was the intervention of the Ugandan army shortly after the outbreak of violence on December 15–16. With the targeted killings of Nuers in Juba and the instant mobilization of former Nuer militias to join the rebellion of Riek Machar, the mood among the Nuer was in favor of revenge killings. Had the so-called White Army not been intercepted by the Ugandan forces as it approached Juba, massacres of a genocidal magnitude would most likely have occurred.

## Regional and International Response to the Crisis

A positive outcome of the Rwandan genocide of 1994 is that the international community has become more alert, proactive, and responsive to situations of conflict that can become genocidal. The basis of this response has been the notion of Sovereignty as Responsibility, which I developed with colleagues in the Africa Project at the Brookings Institution and used as a basis for my dialogue with governments on behalf of IDPs, and which has since evolved into the emerging concept of the Responsibility to Protect. Though controversial, R2P has focused attention on the shared responsibility between the state and the international community for the protection of populations at risk within state borders. Sovereignty is increasingly being recast as responsibility, and the state has the primary responsibility to protect its populations from genocide, war crimes, ethnic cleansing, and crimes against humanity. The international community has the complementary responsibility to assist states to discharge their national responsibility. But should the state be manifestly failing in discharging that responsibility, and should its populations be at risk of massive violence, the international community should assume the obligation to step in to fill the vacuum.

At the time of President Salva Kiir's first attendance at the General Assembly in 2010, I hosted a dinner for him and his delegation that he generously attended, although he was not feeling well. In my brief welcoming statement I said there were two aspects of our culture that were both positive and negative. One was that our people are very egalitarian and each person sees himself or herself as just as good as anyone else. Every family and every group see themselves the same way. I said this was positive as it represents a democratic spirit. But, I said, it made it difficult to govern. My second point was that while the international community was eager to assist, we must be self-reliant and take international support as added value. Then minister of foreign affairs, Nhial Deng Nhial, responded on behalf of the president and underscored this second point.

The case of South Sudan is proving to be one in which the international community has responded positively to the current crisis through the collaboration of the subregional organization, Inter-Governmental Authority for Development (IGAD); the regional organization, the African Union (AU); the international organization, the UN; and other key players. Within a reasonably short time after the outbreak of the violent conflict, they were able to broker an agreement for the cessation of hostilities and start a peace process aimed not only at ending the bloodshed, but also at addressing the root causes and fostering national unity and reconciliation with accountability. While the process is fraught with many challenges, this indicates prospects for mitigating the catastrophe and a promising outcome, although what the precise substantive solution will be remains a matter for debate, dialogue, and conjecture.

Perhaps the real questions that must be posed and answered are the following: How did a people who had struggled for so long to achieve lasting peace and dignity for all allow themselves to fall back into the trap of devastating violence and sharp divisions within the nation? What went wrong and who bears the responsibility for that? How can the root causes be identified and addressed to prevent recurrence? If these and related questions are effectively addressed, that should provide an opportunity in the crisis to pave a constructive path toward lasting peace, stability, and prosperity for all South Sudanese, without discrimination on the basis of their pluralistic ethnic diversity. An aspect of this is the ongoing, ambivalent relationship between Sudan and South Sudan, as well as the interconnection between their internal conflicts, which in turn aggravates the tensions between the two countries.

## Codependent Relationship between the Two Sudans

Although the current crisis in South Sudan may be considered to be purely internal, it is fair to say that it has its roots in the long war between South and North Sudan. It was then that most of the Nuer militias who have now rebelled again with Riek Machar were recruited, trained, armed, and unleashed by the government in Khartoum to fight a proxy war in the South. With the independence of the South, they were granted amnesty, and most of them joined the national army, the Sudan People's Liberation Army, although they were not screened for national service. They remained under their previous commanders and were not fully integrated into the SPLA. During the struggle, rebel movements from the northern states of Southern Kordofan and Blue Nile joined the SPLM/A, thereby blurring the boundaries of the North-South conflict, with the shared objective being the liberation of the whole country and the creation of a New Sudan without discrimination on the grounds of race, ethnicity, religion, culture, or gender. The independence of the South left those Northern allies to continue their struggle within the governance system of the North. Movements in Darfur, which rebelled in 2003, and disgruntled groups in other regions of the Sudan, notably the Beja in the east, and even the Nubians in the far north, share the quest for the vision of a reformed New Sudan.

As a result of these deeply rooted conflicts and unresolved tensions between Sudan and South Sudan, the two countries remain in a codependent relationship involving a complex web of predicaments, being two parts of a country that has been at war with itself for over half a century, and that, even after the Comprehensive Peace Agreement (CPA) of 2005 that led to its partitioning, remains devastated by conflicts within and between the two.

An aspect of these continuing tensions and conflicts is the ambivalence associated with the independence of South Sudan. As is well known, most African countries were created by colonial intervention, which introduced within the new states ethnic, tribal, and regional diversities that were characterized by gross inequalities. While the liberation struggle more or less unified these various identity groups, independence resulted in conflicts over power, access to resources, services, employment, and development opportunities, all now controlled by the center.

After independence, African countries, afraid that diversities and identity-based conflicts would threaten the unity and integrity of the new fragile states, decided that the colonial borders should be made sacrosanct, allegedly to reinforce and preserve national unity and accelerate socioeconomic development. Democratic values, respect for diversity, and protection of human rights were disregarded as luxuries that the fragile states could not afford. It would take decades for the process of liberation struggle from within to be generated, and in many countries, this struggle continues to this day.

It must be emphasized that identity conflicts that can result in geno-cide and mass atrocities are not rooted in mere differences, but rather from the implications of those differences, reflected in gross inequali-ties, discrimination, marginalization, exclusion, and the denial of fun-damental rights. At the core of Sudan's wars that have raged for over half a century lies an acute crisis of national identity. The major aspects of the crisis are the distorted self-perception of the dominant minority group at the center, which, though an African Arab hybrid, sees itself as purely Arab, reinforced by an extremist version of Islam; and the projection of this distorted identity as providing the framework for the identity of a country of immense racial, ethnic, religious, and cultural diversity.

## The Root of Sudan's Crisis of Identity

In Sudan, the historical context of Arabization and Islamization was that if one became a Muslim, spoke Arabic, was culturally Arabized, and could trace or imagine ancestral roots to Arabia, one was elevated to a status of relative dignity; if one was a black and a so-called heathen, one became a legitimate target for enslavement. Despite the existence of non-Arab and non-Muslim groups throughout the country, the main dichotomy was between the Arabized Muslim North and the African South, which was racially, culturally, and religiously indigenously Afri-can. While Arab Islamic assimilation spread in the North, the South developed a contrasting identity of resistance to the Arab Islamic North, which hunted for slaves in the non-Muslim South. The British recog-nized this North-South dichotomy, developed the regions of the North in varying degrees, and generally neglected the South.

As the end of the colonial rule approached, only a few months before the declaration of independence on January 1, 1956, the South, fearful of the consequences of the North taking over power from the British and imposing a system of internal colonialism, staged a rebellion, which escalated into a secessionist war that lasted for seventeen years. The 1972 Addis Ababa Agreement temporarily ended the war by granting the South regional autonomy. The abrogation of that agreement in 1983 led to the resumption of war, not for secession, but for the liberation of the whole country and the creation of a New Sudan of full equality without racial, ethnic, religious, cultural, or gender discrimination.

## Breaking Down the Barriers between the North and the South

The vision of the New Sudan began to inspire the non-Arab groups throughout the country, particularly in the North, and in the mid-1980s these groups joined the South in the struggle. The CPA and the independence of the South left these Northern allies under the domination of the Old Sudan. My visits to Southern Kordofan and Blue Nile just before the January 9, 2011, referendum introduced me to the sense of betrayal by the South that these people felt, even before the independence referendum, although they pledged to continue their own struggle and look to the South for support.

Even then, I realized that this presented a serious dilemma: If the South supported them, the North would destabilize the South and undermine its independence, but abandoning former allies who had contributed enormously to the liberation of the South could not be an honorable option. My reflections during the celebration of Southern independence represented a degree of ambivalence between appreciation for the joy over the South's achievement of a goal for which South Sudanese had struggled and sacrificed so much for so long, and concern over the plight of those left under the domination of the old system, some of whom had stood with the South in the struggle, and without whom the South might not have succeeded.

President Kiir pledged in his independence speech that South Sudan would not abandon its former allies, but would support their cause through peaceful means in cooperation with the North. Kiir's pledge has remained largely symbolic, an aspiration, with at most a discreet, modest support. What I had feared is what is happening: As the former

Northern allies continue their struggle against the central government in Khartoum, the South is alleged, contrary to the stated position of the government of South Sudan, to support them against the objections of the international community, and Sudan is working to destabilize the government of South Sudan by supporting various Southern militias, now including Riek Machar's rebellion.

# Chapter Two: Overlapping Conflicts between the Two Sudans

The three border areas of Abyei, Southern Kordofan (Nuba Mountains), and Blue Nile pose a challenge between Sudan and South Sudan that is potentially both positive and negative. Together, they represent the core of the two countries being bound together by conflicts. Within the framework of a united New Sudan or a separated South, these areas constitute a potential bridge between the North and the South. However, with the Southern secession and persisting conflicts in the neighboring states, the situation becomes more complex. The case of Abyei should be straightforward, since the Abyei Protocol gave the Ngok Dinka the right to decide in six years' time whether to remain in the North or join the South, yet it has been one of the most intractable to resolve. The people of Southern Kordofan and Blue Nile, on the other hand, while given the right to an autonomous status, could only determine their destiny through popular consultation that could only be considered a form of internal self-determination. However, with Southern secession, they could not be content with that status in a country dominated by the Arab Islamic North. It was predictable that they would then either strive to join the South or intensify the struggle for the New Sudan within the North. That apparently has been the case since the independence of the South, a clear indicator of the two countries being bound together by conflicts.

## The Unresolved Contest over Abyei

One of the flashpoints between Sudan and South Sudan is the unresolved problem of the Ngok Dinka in the Abyei area at the North-South border. Abyei has been described, including by the CPA, as a bridge or a strategic link between the North and the South. It was annexed to the North in 1905, although by all criteria, it is part of the South. The areas originally annexed to the North included Twic and Ruweng. These areas were later returned to the South, leaving only the Ngok Dinka under Northern administration. As I later got to know from the former British administrators, there were differences of opinion between those who wanted the Ngok Dinka to be returned to the South and those who wanted them to continue to play a bridging role between the North and the South, a position the Ngok Dinka leadership also favored.

Subsequent British attempts to persuade Paramount Chief Kwol Arob of the Ngok Dinka and later his son, Chief Deng Majok, to rejoin the South were unsuccessful, as the Ngok Dinka leaders saw their bridging role as advantageous to the security of the area. The first war was the beginning of the Ngok Dinka–Missiriya Arab hostility, as the youth of Abyei joined the struggle and the government recruited the Missiriya as militias to fight the South.

The 1972 Addis Ababa Agreement granted the Ngok Dinka the right of self-determination, allowing them to choose between remaining in the North and joining the South, but the government refused to implement those provisions. My proposed plan for the development of Abyei as an autonomous bridging model for peace, unity, and integration also met with skepticism and opposition from various circles. Initially welcomed by the leadership in Khartoum and Juba, it received a hostile response from the authorities in Kordofan, the Missiriya, Southerners, and the majority of the Abyei educated elite, the last of whom strongly identified with the South, and mistakenly saw the proposal as pro-North.

The Ngok Dinka eventually despaired and staged a local rebellion that contributed to the resumption of the North-South war in 1983. The Abyei Protocol of the CPA, the Abyei Boundary Commission (ABC), and the Hague Permanent Court of Arbitration (PCA) demarcated the boundaries of Abyei, but Khartoum blocked their implementation.

Misguided proposals by some ill-informed mediators, prominent among them the special envoy of the United States, General Scott Gration, began to revisit issues that had already been resolved by prior agreements. These second-guessing proposals included the Missiriya voting in the stipulated Abyei referendum, the Missiriya sharing Ngok Dinka administration, and Ngok Dinka ceding more land to the Missiriya beyond what both the ABC and the PCA had demarcated.

## Abyei Boundary Commission Report

Perhaps the most important, but highly controversial, issue was the work of the Abyei Boundary Commission, established pursuant to the Abyei Protocol of the CPA. The ABC reports that after "having duly considered, assessed, and weighed the evidence before them," the experts concluded,

> The Ngok have a legitimate dominant claim to the territory from the Kordofan-Bahr el Ghazal boundary north to latitude 10° 10' N, stretching from the boundary with Darfur to the boundary with Upper Nile, as they were in 1956;
>
> North of latitude 10° 10' N, through the Goz up to and including Tebeldia (north of latitude 10° 35' N) the Ngok and Misseriya share isolated occupation and use rights, dating from at least the condominium period. This gave rise to the shared secondary rights for both the Ngok and Misseriya;
>
> The two parties lay equal claim to the shared areas and accordingly it is reasonable and equitable to divide the Goz between them and locate the northern boundary at a straight line at approximately latitude 10° 22'30" N. The western boundary shall be the Kordofan/Darfur boundary as it was defined on 1 January 1956. The southern boundary shall be the Kordofan-Bahr el-Ghazal-Upper Nile boundary as it was defined on 1st January 1956. The eastern boundary shall extend the line of the Kordofan-Upper Nile boundary at approximately longitude 29°32'15" E, northwards until it meets latitude 10°22'30" N;

The northern and eastern boundaries will be identified and demarcated by a survey team comprising three professional surveyors: one
nominated by the national government of the Sudan, one nominated by
the Government of the Southern Sudan and one international surveyor
nominated by IGAD. The survey team will be assisted by one representative each from the Ngok and Missiriya and two representatives of the
Presidency. The Presidency shall send the nominations for this team to
IGAD for final approval by the international experts;

The Ngok and Missiriya shall retain their established secondary
rights to the use of land north and south of this boundary.

South Sudan accepted the determination of the ABC while Sudan rejected it. Despite the clarity of the Abyei Protocol, the area continues to
face serious problems in the North-South conflict. The Abyei Protocol
provides that, upon the signing of the agreement, Abyei would be accorded a special administrative status under the presidency. That never
happened. The bone of contention remained the report of the ABC. In
his statement to the joint meeting of the cabinet and the Legislative
Assembly of the GoSS on his November 2006 visit to Juba, President
al-Bashir boldly reiterated that the ABC had exceeded its mandate. According to him, the mandate of the ABC was to find the borders of the
nine *omudiat*, or sections, of the Ngok Dinka that existed before their
administration was transferred from Bahr el-Ghazal to Kordofan in
1905, which he said meant identifying the borders of the two provinces. To emphasize that the commission went beyond its mandate, the
president purportedly quoted from the ABC report a sentence in English,
stating, "We failed to find the borders of 1905." Ironically, nowhere in
the ABC report did the members state that they "failed" to find the 1905
borders. What the ABC report did state was that

no map exists showing the area inhabited by the Ngok Dinka in 1905.
Nor is there sufficient documentation produced in that year by Anglo-
Egyptian Condominium government authorities that adequately spell
out the administrative situation that existed in that area at that time.
Therefore, it was necessary for the experts to avail themselves of rele-
vant historical material produced both before and after 1905, as well as

during that year, to determine as accurately as possible the area of the
nine Ngok Dinka chiefdoms as it was in 1905.

The president asserted that, having failed to find the 1905 borders, the
ABC resorted to the borders of 1965, when the Ngok Dinka began to flee
from the area. According to the president, once the commission failed
to find a 1905 map, it should have stopped there and come back to the
negotiating parties for new instructions or actions.

The NCP, the president, and the Missiriya went as far as questioning
the legitimacy of the ABC international experts as foreigners, which they
not only knew and accepted when the ABC was constituted, but indeed
encouraged in order to provide outside neutral expertise. The allegation
that the commission went beyond the mandate and that, as they did not
find a map demarcating the 1905 borders, they should have stopped their
work, was at best a misreading of the mandate and probably a contrived
attempt by those advising the president to discredit the ABC report. Had
there been a map demarcating the borders of the two areas and provinces, there would have been no need for the commission. In fact, British
administrators, such as K. D. D. Henderson and P. P. Howell, who preferred that Abyei not be returned to the administration of Bahr el-Ghazal,
cited the difficulty of determining the borders between the Ngok
Dinka and the Missiriya as the main reason for their position.

Since no map demarcating the Ngok Dinka–Missiriya–Bahr
el-Ghazal–Kordofan borders existed, the mandate of the ABC was to determine the locations where the nine Ngok Dinka sections lived in 1905
and, in the light of their findings, determine and demarcate the borders.
Their mandate was never intended to be a hunt for a map already demarcating the borders, which everyone knew did not exist. The commission therefore used various scientific methods, which they elaborately
describe in their report, and reached the conclusion that in 1905 the
Ngok Dinka were living in the same areas they occupied until they were
forced to flee by the North-South conflict that first extended to the area
in 1965. They also confirmed a point British administrators in the
area and other observers always noted, that apart from the areas of
primary occupation by the Ngok Dinka and the Missiriya, there is a "no-
man's land," which they shared. That was the area the commission

divided evenly between the Ngok Dinka and the Missiriya. A careful reading of the report cannot fail to impress the reader that the commission members performed a thorough, professional, and objective collection and analysis of evidence to reach their conclusions and determinations. They themselves had not the slightest doubt about their objectivity, the fairness of their findings, or their judgment.

Their foreign identity, which was now being invoked against them, was initially seen as a guarantee of neutrality and objectivity. Even the fact that they did not submit their report to the parties in the commission, which was now being used against them, was based on the parties' agreement on the procedure for overcoming predictable deadlock. What was obvious was that the Northern interest groups, the president included, decided to construct an arbitrary argument to hold to and to give it a semblance of legitimacy by their persistence and intransigence. In holding to their position unabashedly, they were encouraged by the fact that despite the outcry of the SPLM, the GoSS, and President Salva Kiir, there was nothing they could do to effectively challenge Sudan, short of going back to war, for which no one had an appetite.

Although I knew members of the ABC personally, I chose not to contact them in order to avoid any impression that I was exerting influence on them. When they presented their report to the presidency, which comprised President Omar al-Bashir; the newly appointed first vice president, John Garang de Mabior; and Vice President Ali Osman Mohamed Taha, Garang later told me that the president responded by observing that the government should expect a rebellion from the Missiriya. Garang reacted by saying that such a rebellion would be their joint responsibility to confront and not for President Bashir alone. John Garang requested that I arrange a meeting with the Missiriya leaders, but to do it in such a way that the request for the meeting came from them. I succeeded in arranging that scenario, but the meeting was aborted by the NCP authorities once they learned about it. It became obvious that there was a hidden agenda regarding Abyei.

In a statement to a Washington think tank in February 2007, a senior member of the NCP admitted that the real issue in Abyei was to which side the oil wealth in the area would go. He later intimated to me that if the country were sure to remain united, Abyei would not be a problem. Ironically, the Missiriya were becoming acutely divided, with a few of their elites in Khartoum toeing the NCP line, while most of the people on the ground, including their traditional leaders, were openly complaining about having been exploited by the NCP in its war with the South, without any benefits accruing to them, and they were seeking ways of restoring their traditional peaceful coexistence and cooperation with the Ngok Dinka. Toward that end, they held a series of meetings, both in the area and in Khartoum. They also joined the Ngok Dinka in calling for the return of the displaced populations to their areas of origin, which extended as far north as the Blue Line, south of the shared area demarcated by the ABC.

## Sudan's Demand for a Shared Dinka-Missiriya Administration in Abyei

President al-Bashir concluded his November statement regarding Abyei by restating his position in favor of a *joint* Dinka-Missiriya administration under the presidency. It was well known that there was no legal or historical foundation for such an idea. To the contrary, history demonstrated that the Abyei area, comprising the nine sections, had always been administered as a separate entity, even after it had been incorporated into the Dar el Missiriya Rural Council/District, later elevated to a province. Abyei Town was then shrewdly chosen by the Kordofan authorities to be the headquarters of the district in order to undermine the political aspirations of the Ngok Dinka toward the South and to lay a ground for claiming the land as Northern. And nothing was done to develop Abyei as the headquarters.

Even in matters relating to the administration of justice, Abyei was the only area in the North that was governed by the 1931 Chiefs' Courts Ordinance, which applied to the South, instead of the 1932 Native Courts Ordinance, which was applicable to the North. That allowed Ngok Dinka chiefs to administer justice in accordance with their own customary laws, which were more in conformity with those prevailing in the South.

Following the 2008 invasion of Abyei by Khartoum, the parties agreed to submit their conflict over the ABC to the International Court of Arbitration (ICA) for reconsideration. The court's decision was to be final and binding. The ICA revised the determination of the ABC by awarding about 40 percent of the territory the ABC had determined as Ngok Dinka land to the North. Despite the loss of their land, the Ngok Dinka and the GoSS accepted the determination of the ICA. Khartoum also accepted the decision but never cooperated with its implementation. Instead, it began to set new contentions for Abyei and the self-determination referendum, such as insisting that the Missiriya share in the interim administration of the Ngok Dinka on an equal basis with the Ngok Dinka and vote in the self-determination referendum of the Ngok Dinka.

Confirming this historical background to the Ngok Dinka administration, the ABC report stated, "The record shows that the Ngok were administered separately," and set forth the evidence supporting that statement. The report went on to say, "the Ngok retained their identity and control over the local affairs and maintained a separate court system and hierarchy of chiefs." According to the Abyei Protocol of the CPA, the establishment of the special administrative status in the area was not contingent on the determination of the borders between the Ngok Dinka and the Missiriya, but merely on the *presentation* of the ABC report. Section 5.2 of the Protocol states, "Upon presentation of the final report, the Presidency shall take necessary action to put the special administrative status of Abyei Area into immediate effect." Since the ABC report was to be "final and binding," no dispute was anticipated over its determination. The position of the NCP and the president, challenging not only the findings and determination of the ABC, but also the foreign identity of the experts, was a unilateral and arbitrary disregard for the agreed-upon rules of the game.

Because of the Sudan government's stand, the sensitive area of Abyei remained without administration, virtually stateless, a state of affairs that discouraged agencies from delivering services. Some agencies and nongovernmental organizations (NGOs) were, however, beginning to respond to the needs of the area and were operating in the areas demarcated by the ABC as part of the main occupation of the Ngok Dinka. Some nongovernmental organizations were also being accused of favoring the Missiriya in the provision of services, avoiding operating in Ngok Dinka areas, and toeing the government line, including advocating the

Northern proposal for a joint Dinka-Missiriya administration in Abyei. Oil companies were also reportedly discriminating against the Ngok Dinka, employing only the Arabs, providing them with services, and encouraging them to settle and farm in areas well within Ngok Dinka territory.

The Missiriya were allegedly being compensated by the oil companies for the exploitation of the land of the Ngok Dinka. In addition, there had been incidents of violence against the Ngok Dinka involving government-supported Southern militias and elements from the Missiriya.

The lack of administration in Abyei meant that the area was, according to the special representative of the secretary-general, "without any formal policing, public sanitation or health services." Coordination for much-needed security in the area was absent, and the area was not receiving any services from the presidency or the Government of National Unity (GoNU), nor the 2 percent of the revenues from the oil production in the area that was stipulated by the Abyei Protocol. Even the way station that was promised by the UN never materialized. Furthermore, while international humanitarian and development agencies wanted to assist in the area, the vacuum of administration inhibited their involvement.

What was particularly disturbing about the situation in Abyei was that one side of what should be a collegiate presidency was holding the other side hostage by taking a rigid and uncompromising position, without any apparent pressure from anywhere to move matters forward.

Fortunately, the GoSS, in cooperation with the Ngok Dinka community leaders, and especially the tribal chiefs, continued to explore ways of filling the administrative vacuum. The GoSS and the SPLM eventually succeeded in doing so by establishing a strong presence in Abyei and providing support to the tribal chiefs. That encouraged the displaced populations to return to their areas of origin and became the only avenue open to the international community to provide badly needed relief and social services to assist the returnees in reintegrating and stabilizing themselves in the area. Efforts by the GoSS and the SPLM office in Abyei needed to be vigorously supported. After all, Salva Kiir, as a partner in what was envisaged as a joint presidency, could not be held hostage by the blatant refusal of one part of the presidency to comply with the CPA. Again, these promising signals never fully materialized, and Abyei remained abandoned, with limited but much appreciated support by the government of South Sudan.

Ultimately, the responsibility to find a solution to this crisis had to be assumed by a united presidency. Salva Kiir, in his opening statement at the joint meeting of the NCP and the SPLM, highlighted the Abyei crisis as a threat to the CPA, and he was reported to have later told al-Bashir that there could be no partnership between their respective parties without a solution to the Abyei problem.

The NCP-SPLM Joint Political Committee that was organized to follow up on the issue held meetings, but it did not come up with new ideas for resolving the impasse. The position of the SPLM was to resort to alternative measures. What those were was never entirely clear, but they most likely entailed moving forward with creating its own version of an Abyei administration, which the GoSS had indeed already done. Since the Abyei Protocol classified the inhabitants of Abyei as joint citizens of the neighboring Northern and Southern states of Southern Kordofan and Bahr el-Ghazal (now Warrap), respectively, such a move was considered by the people of Abyei and by the GoSS as justifiable under the Abyei Protocol. It was also argued that since the presidency was supposed to be joint, which should give the president (NCP) and the first vice president (SPLM) equal say in making presidential decisions, it was contrary to the spirit and letter of the CPA for the president to exclude the first vice president and make his own decisions. That action then justified the first vice president and GoSS to take their own action to fulfill their part of the obligations under the Abyei Protocol. It was therefore expected that unless the collegiate presidency could come to a consensus on Abyei, the SPLM and the GoSS should move forward to establish their own component of the Abyei administration, financed in the interim by the GoSS, until the boundary issue was resolved.

An intriguing development, however, was that the people of Abyei decided to take matters into their own hands by establishing an administration, run by the indigenous NGO, the Abyei Development Committee (ADC), in cooperation with the traditional authorities. On January 14, 2007, Ngok Dinka students and community leaders occupied the former NCP civil administration office and, after intervention by the police, the keys were given to the ADC. Despite the fact that this ad hoc administration was not formalized and had no legal status, that local initiative encouraged the people of the area to be self-reliant and to develop their own model of indigenous governance and self-generated development. In the view of some observers, that was perhaps the only initiative of its kind in Sudan, and it stood the chance of encouraging people to develop their local capacities.

Although the failure of the presidency to implement the Abyei Protocol and the recommendations of the ABC report was a discouraging factor in the return of the displaced population, Abyei was acknowledged as the area to which there were large IDP returns. This was mostly spontaneous and unassisted, as the UN was shying away from assisting in the Ngok Dinka return to the Abyei area. So, Abyei was once again besieged and isolated, with forces of the SAF and the SPLA heavily deployed North and South of Abyei town.

## Peaceful Co-existence

On my visit to Khartoum and Juba in October 2005, the issue of Abyei again figured prominently in my discussions with the authorities, including First Vice President Salva Kiir, Vice President Ali Osman Taha, and other senior officials. Taha told me that they needed my help on the Abyei issue. My position in the discussions with the authorities and the Missiriya was to emphasize the importance of upholding the report of the ABC, and I argued that fiddling with it would open doors for fiddling with other aspects of the CPA. But, given the different reactions to the report, creative ways had to be found to overcome the impasse and move forward with the implementation of the Abyei Protocol. One way of moving forward was to encourage the two communities to engage in a dialogue on ways to coexist peacefully and cooperate in sharing the resources of the area, irrespective of the boundaries demarcation.

There were, of course, obvious reasons why the findings of the ABC were not viewed favorably by the Missiriya. First, the division of the land, with the prospects of Abyei joining the South and the South voting for independence, made their access to survival resources such as water and grazing lands seem less secure to them. Such access was, however, guaranteed by the Abyei Protocol and reaffirmed by the ABC report. Even the Interim Constitution of Southern Sudan (ICSS) stated that "customary seasonal access rights to land shall be respected." Any efforts by the key parties to remind and reassure the Missiriya of these protections might help allay their fears.

Second, since Sudan's independence, the Missiriya had enjoyed the status of a favored group, with racial, ethnic, religious, and cultural affinities with successive rulers in the central government. The impartiality with which foreign rulers managed their relations ended with independence. Should the Ngok Dinka join the South, it would mean that the Missiriya would lose their favored status. Arguably, however, the emphasis on preserving this special affinity with the center was fading as the Missiriya began to closely examine the benefits that affinity had failed to bring them. While the government's position on Abyei was allegedly in defense of the Missiriya interests, there were increasing signs of disillusionment on the part of the Missiriya, who perceived themselves as being exploited by the NCP government for its own political purposes or to protect its ambitions for the oil reserves in the region. This accusation was strongly voiced by a number of Missiriya during a joint meeting with Ngok Dinka, which I convened in Khartoum in November 2006. A report by one NGO field researcher, who held meetings with Missiriya leaders during their dry-season camps in Ngok Dinka territory, confirmed the same theme of complaint. According to the report, "[The Missiriya] kept emphasizing that they and the Dinka are brothers. . . . They are fed up with the NCP. They kept referring to the 2% they were supposed to get!! Where is it? They repeatedly asked. Abdala, the Missiriya representative, said that after the fighting, they have received nothing. They feel exploited."

Third, it is a truism that no one who is dominant in a unity framework would easily welcome the break-up of such unity, since it means the loss of dominion. The fact that the Ngok Dinka were joined to an administration in which the Missiriya predominated reinforced their hegemony.

Fourth, the loss of territory would also imply the loss of the resources associated with the land, traditionally reflected in water and pastures, but now intensified by the raised stakes in the oil resources and revenues.

As noted earlier, in the context of an increased Missiriya disillusionment with the NCP and a desire to revive and return to their traditional ways of reconciling differences and living together peacefully, the Ngok Dinka and the Missiriya initiated ongoing dialogue with one another, even prior to the CPA. Missiriya leaders also initiated meetings with me during my visits to the country with the goal of improving relations between them and the Ngok Dinka. Those meetings were attended by Ngok Dinka community leaders in Khartoum.

Although the Missiriya favored being left alone with the Ngok Dinka to discuss their differences and find local solutions, and the Ngok Dinka resisted any group discussions aimed at negotiating the Abyei Protocol and the ABC report, both agreed on the urgent need for the Ngok Dinka to return to their home areas in Abyei and establish their own administration in the area, and for the two peoples to restore their erstwhile peaceful coexistence and cooperation. They also agreed to continue their dialogue on the issues dividing them locally.

In terms of local peace building, the Abyei Protocol required the presidency, "as a matter of urgency," to "start peace and reconciliation process for Abyei." In the absence of support by the ruling NCP and the GoS for such initiatives, political entrepreneurs or middlemen derived personal gain by posing as the representatives of the local Arab communities to pursue the policies of the government. In reality, these people were perceived by the local Arab communities as self-seeking, and, far from serving the best interest of their people, they were merely fanning intertribal tensions and hostilities that were detrimental to the long-term interests of the people. Ironically, most, if not all, of these individuals were not even from the communities immediately neighboring the Ngok Dinka. Some of them were in fact from the far north, completely unconnected to the local context and concerns. Since reaping the benefits from the collaboration with the SPLM, the Missiriya became increasingly interested in a local solution with the Ngok Dinka and even in a closer relationship with the SPLM/A. In fact, it was reported that significant numbers of Missiriya had asked to join the SPLA. As neither the Missiriya nor the Ngok Dinka were receiving their

2 percent share of the oil revenue from the Abyei area, as provided for in the Abyei Protocol of the CPA, the failure to implement the Abyei Protocol was in fact hurting them both.

Although the quest for Dinka-Missiriya reconciliation remains a pressing priority for the two communities, the assassination of the Ngok Dinka paramount chief, Kwol Deng Kwol, on May 4, 2013, has become a major complicating factor that has enormously strained Dinka-Missiriya relations. And yet, even the late Chief Kwol, who was strongly committed to dialogue, peace, and reconciliation, would tell his people that his death should not be an obstacle to peace and reconciliation with the Missiriya. Abyei clearly remains a treacherous link between the North and the South and a symbol of both positive and negative potentials between the two countries.

## Southern Kordofan and Blue Nile

Although the border areas of Southern Kordofan and Blue Nile did not share problems of the magnitude of those of Abyei, they also represented challenges to North-South relations. The implementation of the CPA in the two areas was moving very slowly, generating considerable frustration from the SPLM/A and the local population. A senior SPLM official from the Nuba Mountains of Southern Kordofan was reported to have complained, "We fought for 20 years, and now have seven paid positions in the State Government. Is that what we fought for? With no change and no peace dividends, people will go back to war." An SPLM leader from the area also said to me, "These areas are time bombs in Sudanese politics. Up to now, as we are sitting here, there is nothing that has moved forward in this agreement."

As long as Sudan remained united, those regions could offer crosscutting alliances between the South and marginalized regions of the North. Branches of the SPLM in the North were already in place to play that role, and enrollment there was popular, at one point causing concern in the South that the party might be taken over by Northerners. In discussing Southern fears of a Northern takeover of the SPLM, the late John Garang told me, "These are the fears of a people who have been dominated for far too long." It was predictable that if the South opted for secession, as was expected, the role of those regions would become even more complex. They might consider choosing between joining the South, through the expansion of the consultations process, which was unlikely, and intensifying the struggle for the New Sudan in the North, which was the most probable. The prospects of reunification between the North and the South, should the New Sudan agenda succeed in the North, would provide an added incentive for crosscutting collaboration. These areas are therefore central to the theme of the two countries being bound together by conflicts and the prospects of their resolution.

"The vision of the Movement was about the whole Sudan, and it was about change," a prominent SPLM leader from the region told me. "By virtue of the marginalized coming together, they have broadened the core bases and foundation for change in the country. So, I wouldn't imagine that the interests of the South are still separate." He warned of the consequences, should the South abandon those areas: "If the South wants to go, it must work very hard to pull these areas away from the North. . . . And these people are ready to go with the South. They have been given the opportunity to address this in Parliament, and I believe they will do so. . . . But if the agreement is not going to be implemented as it is, then they will opt for a bigger consultation mechanism . . . up to self-determination." In his view, if the South did not support the cause of these areas, they would give very dangerous ammunition to the North. "The disadvantaged areas can be effectively used to destabilize the South more than before. If they get excluded, the situation can be unstable."

The minister of culture and social affairs of Blue Nile State was reported to have threatened that his state would join the South if the provision of the CPA pertaining to popular consultation was not properly implemented. He was also reported to have warned that if the South seceded, the people of Blue Nile and the Nuba Mountains would form a New South in the North and that they could count on the backing of the independent South. The success or failure of the arrangements in these two border regions could have a significant effect on the prospects for the arrangements in Darfur and the East.

It is worth noting that the 2006 peace agreement in Darfur was in significant measure facilitated by the SPLM representatives in the talks, notably Malik Agar of Southern Blue Nile, Dr. Barnaba Marial Benjamin, Dr. Lual Deng, and Yasser Arman. I had the opportunity to be in Abuja during the last crucial phases of the talks, and I was able to have discussions with President Olusegun Obasanjo of Nigeria, leaders of the rebel movements (Abdel Wahid Mohamed Ahmed Nour and Minni Minawi) and members of their negotiating teams, Vice President Ali Osman Mohamed Taha and members of his Sudan government delegation, members of the U.S. delegation, and resource persons of the AU mediation team. I was informed by Vice President Taha that the role of the SPLM representatives was crucial in that they assured the Darfur leaders of their support for their cause and the commonalities in the objectives of their respective liberation struggles. My discussions with the Darfur leaders, which were attended by the SPLM representatives, also revealed strong solidarity between the two regional groups.

## Security Concerns

The main complaint in both areas was that an unpredictable security situation prevailed. The NCP fueled animosities between Arab and non-Arab tribes, and increased uncertainty about the future of the border states after the 2011 referendum in the South.

In Southern Kordofan, integration of forces (the Joint Integrated Units [JIUs]) was reportedly slow. The NCP authorities were said to have resisted the integration of the police and civil service in the area on the grounds that it was not provided for in the agreement. According to a senior SPLM official, while their party considered all armed groups other than the SPLA to be "other armed groups" (OAGs) under the CPA, the NCP had various groups that it refused to recognize as OAGs. President al-Bashir was reported to have said that no one abolished the Popular Defense Forces (PDF) and that no one could abolish them. As a result, the security situation in the area remained tense. The response of the police to recurring incidents of insecurity resulting from Arab attacks on the Nuba was said to have been very deficient. I was told that when the Nuba were killed by the Arabs, the SAF would not move, and the Arab-dominated police would not respond. And when people complained, the authorities insisted on written complaints, which, for a largely illiterate society, was a restriction. But even with written complaints, the police would not follow up. In one specific case at a place north of Dilling, it was reported that an Arab tribal group gathered to attack, and, although the police were informed, they only advanced toward the scene within a certain distance, but stopped short of going to the area of the attacking group. It was what one source described as "lazy implementation." The inequality between the Nuba and the Arabs was striking in the differing compensation (*dia*) for homicide, which was said to be thirty cows for an Arab and half that number for a Nuba.

The security situation was also not helped by the increased support being given by the NCP to Arab tribes and militias in the area. It was reported that the NCP had built up competitive tribal groupings, rendering support to Arab tribes against the non-Arabs. It was alleged that in criminal cases, whenever people filed complaints against groups that were supported and controlled by the NCP, no action was taken. Overall, the NCP was said to be afraid that the unity of non-Arab tribes would be directed against the Arabs and was therefore striving to "divide and conquer" the non-Arabs in hopes of ensuring solidarity with the North, regardless of the result of the 2011 referendum.

## Uncertainty about the Political Future

The expected outcome of the self-determination referendum in the South and the uncertainty surrounding the states' future were on the minds of Blue Nile and Southern Kordofan residents. The view generally held in these areas and in the South was that if the future of these areas was not determined to the satisfaction of the people, and should the South decide to secede, local rebellions could bring the war back to the South and might well lead to the fragmentation of the country beyond these two Northern regions. The implications of Southern independence for the country, and the sustainability of that independence, would most likely be determined by the response of these areas, not only after the referendum, but even before.

Ideally, what the people of these regions wished for was not for the South to secede, or for them to join an independent South, but for all the marginalized regions to continue to pursue the SPLM vision of a New Sudan. While the CPA-stipulated popular consultation gave them something to fall back on, they were not sure what it meant exactly, or what the end result would be. What they emphasized with a remarkable degree of consistency was that they would not accept continued domination by the Arab North. On their part, the mostly Arab people of Western Kordofan, which was annexed to Southern Kordofan, were demanding the restoration of their state. The general view among the non-Arab population was that the stipulated popular consultation, which would be exercised through an elected assembly, should determine whether the area remained in the North, and under what arrangement, or join the South, should it vote in favor of secession. Should the South secede, some favored joining it, either through the popular consultation or through armed struggle, while others favored continuing to struggle for the New Sudan, hopefully with the support of the South.

## Comparing the Race Relations in the Two Areas

While the situation in the two regions was almost identical, it was reported that the intensity of ethnic or intertribal conflicts found in Southern Kordofan did not appear to exist in Blue Nile. As a senior SPLM official in the state explained to me, Blue Nile had "no racial problems, no ethnic problems, no differences of any kind." There had been, however, complaints by some groups regarding the lack of inclusiveness in the state government.

In both states, cooperation between the parties in the implementation of the CPA was reported to be poor, and the NCP continuously obstructed attempts to harmonize the civil service and the law enforcement agents. According to the authorities I interviewed, the police were not integrated, the JIUs had not been fully formed, and the SAF remained in the area in large numbers.

Perhaps the issue about which people in both states expressed the strongest feelings was what would become of their area if the South should decide to secede. There was said to be overwhelming support for the SPLM/A, and it was thought that the separation of the South could lead to the disintegration of the rest of the country. Their interpretation of popular consultation was that the marginalized areas of the North would continue to struggle for the New Sudan, even if the South seceded. But there was a tendency to dismiss the possibility of the South seceding. One leading SPLM member noted that the movement was seen as a father by all marginalized regions of the North, and a father does not abandon his child, however bad the child might be.

In any case, they argued, Blue Nile and Southern Kordofan were too intertwined with the South to be separated. They said that their troops were part of the SPLA forces serving in the South and the North and that they were part of the SPLM at all levels. They did not see how separation could be possible. Of all the people I spoke with, only the *wali* (governor), an NCP member, reported that the people of Blue Nile had made it clear to their negotiating team at Naivasha that they would not join the South. The real issue for the people, however, did not seem to be joining the South; it was, rather, an issue of continuing the struggle for a New Sudan, hopefully with the support of the South.

# Chapter Three: Safeguarding a Precarious Peace

## Final Steps toward the CPA

During my visits to Sudan, I always engaged in consultation with a wide variety of people, including the leadership at the highest levels. Before the CPA was concluded, I met with Dr. John Garang in Nairobi at a time when there was pressure for him to meet with the first vice president, Ali Osman Mohamed Taha, which he was resisting. He posed the rhetorical question, "What will he tell me that their negotiators have not said or will not say?" Nevertheless, Garang intimated to me that in his view, this was the right regime with which to negotiate an agreement, because, as he put it, the government was weak and likely to concede more than a strong government would.

In my subsequent meetings with President Omar al-Bashir and First Vice President Ali Osman Taha, separately, both men expressed the view that they did not think Garang was interested in peace or ready to negotiate in good faith. I surprised them by stressing that I had just met with Garang and that, for reasons I did not need to get into, he had expressed the view that the regime was the right party with which to negotiate a peace accord. Both appeared surprised, but pleased to hear that.

As though he had intuited the hidden reasons Garang had given me, al-Bashir confided to me that some people considered the regime weak. "How can we be weak when we have successfully withstood the opposition of the world against us?" he asked rhetorically. "Even Arab and Muslim countries were hostile to us. Now, they are all coming around to enter into more positive relations with us." It was as though he wanted me to convey the message back to Garang that the regime was not as weak as he might think.

At the end of the meeting with Taha, he informed me that the hoped-for meeting with Garang had in fact been arranged and that he would leave the following day for Nairobi for the meeting. Initially, Taha simply announced, "I am going to meet with your friend." I wondered who that was, which is when Taha disclosed that it was Garang. That was indicative of the fact that the authorities considered me close to John Garang and felt they could use that connection in their efforts to connect with him. In fact, that much had already been disclosed to me by the foreign minister, Dr. Mustafa Osman Ismail. Dr. Ismail, however, explained that there were conflicting views between, on the one hand, those who wanted to cooperate with Garang's opponents in the South in an effort to build up alternative leadership so that Garang should not be seen as the sole representative of the South, and, on the other hand, those who preferred to cooperate with people like me on the grounds that, though a nonpartisan and objective participant, I was known to have a good personal relationship with Garang. Taha's reference to me as Garang's friend was therefore an echo of a view widely held in the official Northern circles and also among Southerners. Indeed, it was quite well known that I was one of the few Southerners who shared Garang's vision of a new, united, restructured Sudan—at least that was what most Southerners told me.

## Principles for Evaluating the CPA Implementation

At the time of my undertaking the assessment of the CPA implementation, I considered four factors to be central: the extent to which peace was consolidated and a resumption of hostilities avoided, the development of mutual confidence between the NCP and SPLM in the credibility of implementation, the actions taken to make unity attractive to the

South, and the predictions on how the South would vote at the self-determination referendum in 2011. A year into the CPA implementation, peace was precariously holding; the parties were striving to forge an ambivalent and fragile partnership in the implementation process; but, contrary to original stipulation and expectation, there were no indications that unity was being made attractive, and the prediction therefore was that the South would almost certainly opt for secession. And yet, ironically, although apparently not fully realized by the parties at the time, the two countries would remain connected, and paradoxically bound together, by conflicts within and between them by proxy.

While peace was holding, divergent considerations still appeared to be guiding the parties in their uneasy alliance. For the SPLM, the CPA had to be made to work to ensure that the self-determination referendum was not jeopardized. For the NCP, the CPA enabled the party to pursue its economic interests, its continued dominance over the politics of North Sudan, and its Arab Islamic agenda, with minimum concessions. From this vantage point, the NCP had no interest in making unity attractive to the South. Should the referendum result in Southern independence, it could be a blessing in disguise, as it would remove a chronic obstacle to the realization of the Northern Arab Islamic vision for the country. Within this spectrum, the SPLM vision of a New (United) Sudan, freed from the historic discrimination based on race, ethnicity, religion, culture, or gender, became merely wishful thinking that was not being pursued in earnest.

While unity ceased to be a priority for the CPA partners, there were regional (both African and Arab) and international actors who still preferred to see Sudan remain united for a variety of reasons, partly geopolitical and partly economic. Indeed, for the same reason that the NCP viewed unity as obstructive, the South had been a moderating factor against pressures to turn Sudan into an Arab Islamic state.

If the creation of a New Sudan remained a goal worth pursuing from a regional and international perspective, it was incumbent upon regional and international actors to play a strategic role in promoting it and making unity an attractive option for the South. Nor should the rhetorical commitment of the SPLM to the vision of a New Sudan be taken lightly, as strategic alliances had already been established with the marginalized regions of the North that would most likely continue to have an impact on Southern Sudanese outlook. Even if the South were to separate, it could be expected to remain engaged in the struggle of these regions to reform and transform the governance system in the North. This, indeed, is one of the principal elements of the paradox of being bound together by conflicts. John Garang had always argued that even if the goal of the South was independence from the North, only by transforming the system in the North would they guarantee Southern independence. By the same token, the Arab Islamic regime in Khartoum can only feel secure by having a regime in the South that poses no threat to them and their ideology.

From the perspective of the South and those who supported the SPLM/A vision for the country, several lines of action were needed to advance the vision of a New Sudan, whatever the ultimate outcome of the self-determination referendum in the South. As I saw them then, these included the following.

First, the GoSS needed to be supported to be a strong and effective constitutional democracy that would be respectful of international standards of good governance and provide an alternative model to the old (NCP-led) Sudan. An aspect of this support must be robust programs of reconstruction and development that would provide tangible peace dividends. Infrastructural development, in particular the construction of road networks and information communications technology within the South and linking the region with the North, could significantly reinforce the potential for political and economic cooperation between the two regions, whether the country remained administratively united or was divided.

Second, the SPLA, as the national army of the South, had to be supported to become a well-trained, well-equipped, professional force capable of ensuring the security of South Sudan and deterring major violations of the CPA. Such a force, even without direct interference in the conflicts of the North, could continue to be a source of inspiration and moral support for the marginalized areas of the North in their struggle against the discriminating system of the Old Sudan. Unfortunately, with the absorption of former militias that were not fully integrated into the SPLM/A, the army became too large (in the words of an expert–"obese"—both in numbers and in overweight commanders). The army was also fragmented, tribalized, unprofessional, and ill equipped to defend the nation. Instead, buying peace became an unbearable burden on the economy. This also meant that the deterrence against the North was no longer tenable.

Third, the SPLM needed to be built up as a party and supported to be effective throughout the country as the principal proponent of the vision of a New Sudan, and to play an effective role in the midterm national elections that could change the course of politics in the country. Even more than the SPLA, the SPLM should continue to be a source of inspiration and support for the marginalized areas of the North, especially through its Northern branch, whatever the outcome of the referendum in the South, again by either setting conditions for political and economic cooperation between North and South, or, failing that, promoting unity by conflict.

Fourth, crosscutting alliances, especially between the SPLM and other political forces in the North, needed to be encouraged and supported to break down the North-South barriers and cultivate a national platform for the evolution of the New Sudan. This had to include broad-based, people-to-people contacts and dialogue through visits, conferences, and workshops to discuss the differences and explore common grounds for building the New Sudan.

Fifth, efforts needed to be made to win the cooperation of the NCP in the transformation of the system to become more respectful and protective of diversity. The stated objective need not be to force the NCP out of power, but to join the national consensus behind the formation of a New Sudan of pluralism and democratic transformation toward equality. The strategy should be to reward the party for positive policy changes, while engaging it in a constructive dialogue to accelerate reforms in the areas where they were needed. Should the process of reform result in a democratic regime change, it would at least be in an environment of national reconciliation, unity, and harmony, without acrimony, vengeance, or vindictiveness.

Sixth, the West, in particular the United States, needed to adopt a less ambivalent or equivocal involvement with Sudan and become more actively engaged to help influence developments toward the policy objectives of a New Sudan. This would require reassessing the form and level of diplomatic relations and the sanctions regime. A full diplomatic representation in Khartoum, with a strong presence also in Juba, could significantly enhance a constructive and potentially productive engagement. As the issue of sanctions was a more debatable and divisive one, the way forward might be to phase the resolution of the problem. The first phase would have been to exempt the GoSS from the sanctions, in addition to the humanitarian and other areas already exempt. The second, perhaps incremental, phase would have been to engage in substantial discussions with the GoNU to identify those areas where they had made progress and deserved recognition and reward, and those areas where reforms were still needed, which would have been equally rewarded if and when they were made.

Needless to say, these objectives were not pursued in earnest, and far less achieved. However, elements of these objectives remain pertinent, especially in the context of the two countries, now separated, yet bound together by conflicts.

At the time of my field visits in April and June 2006, the parties appeared to have a mutual interest in preserving peace and avoiding a return to war. From the perspective of the NCP, the CPA offered them a degree of legitimacy that had been lacking previously. It allowed the party to continue with its Arab Islamic agenda in the North, afforded the North 50 percent of the oil revenues from the South, and provided the first real opportunity since independence for peace and security and prospects for development and nation building. It also offered the opportunity of improving relations with the Western powers, in particular, the United States. The CPA had endorsed the NCP Arab Islamic agenda in the North. The partially accepted Darfur Peace Agreement, had it not unraveled, would also have ensured the containment of that region. The Eastern Sudan Peace Agreement was also likely to enable the NCP to contain the Eastern Front. Sustaining this containment required making tactical compromises, without undue risks to the Arab Islamic agenda.

From the perspective of the SPLM, what was crucial was that the agreement held until the referendum in 2011. While they must strive for credibility in the implementation process, they should not allow any failures or flaws to jeopardize the referendum. However, Southerners were prepared to go back to war, should a major violation threaten their vital interests under the CPA, of which the right of self-determination was the most fundamental. Indeed, a widely shared view among Southerners was that the return to war was quite likely, if not inevitable, because of past experiences with too many dishonored agreements— in the words of Abel Alier's book, *South Sudan: Too Many Agreements Dishonored*.

In this context, making unity attractive did not come across as an objective of interest to the parties. The goal of a New United Sudan was at best a rhetorical vision that tended to be associated with the late SPLM/A leader, Dr. John Garang de Mabior. Nevertheless, though not initially supportive of the New Sudan vision, Garang's successor, Salva Kiir, was increasingly articulating the New Sudan vision with an elevated sense of commitment. This indicates the extent to which Garang's vision was becoming popular among the Southerners after his death, more so than when he was alive. It also provided a sustainable basis for securing alliances and support from the marginalized Northern regions and opposition groups as well as from the countries of the region and the international community. This is a core feature of a nation bound by conflict to remain paradoxically both divided and united.

In light of these paradoxes, and the history of dishonored agreements and numerous incidents of noncompliance that had already been demonstrated by the NCP, there was increasing concern that the exercise of the right of self-determination by the South might not be as guaranteed as originally assumed. It was a well-known fact that Northerners, including leading members of the NCP, appeared divided on their acceptance of the CPA, with some believing that it had given the South far too much, disadvantaging the North and making it increasingly vulnerable to uncompromising demands from other regions in the aggrieved periphery. More than one official described President Bashir, and to some extent the NCP, as under siege. This might account for Bashir's hardline response to international involvement in Darfur, which was seen as inspired by the achievements of the Southern struggle.

## Elements of CPA Implementation

Most observers agreed at the time of my study on the process of the CPA implementation that there had been commendable progress on a number of issues and that the agreement had thus far proven durable and effective in preventing major hostilities. In the joint meeting between the NCP and the SPLM, the parties reaffirmed their partnership and commitment to the implementation of the CPA "in letter and spirit." Those aspirations notwithstanding, the widely shared view was that the CPA had yet to produce a sincere partnership between the ruling parties.

Nevertheless, impressive achievements had been made in many areas, notably, the adoption of the Interim National Constitution (INC), the Interim Constitution of Southern Sudan, and most of the state constitutions; and the formation of the GoNU, the GoSS, and state governments—including the establishment of their respective legislative assemblies and numerous committees and commissions. These achievements were, however, clouded by delays, mistrust, lack of transparency, acrimonious exchanges between the ruling parties, and allegations of numerous actions considered inconsistent with the CPA and the INC.

While the areas of concern in the implementation process were many, in his opening statement to the NCP-SPLM joint conference, Salva Kiir listed "the most burning issues," including the following: the delay in the adoption of the ABC report and the establishment of an administration in accordance with the CPA; the slow and unmonitored withdrawal of forces and the delay in the formation of JIUs; the delay in the North-South 1956 boundary demarcation, considering that the provisions on wealth sharing and security arrangements could not be implemented satisfactorily until the border was determined and demarcated; questions pertaining to the accuracy of the oil revenue accounts and SPLM and GoSS access to the existing contracts, participation in the determination of the oil produced in each well drilled in South Sudan, measurement processes of oil in transportation and export, sale and auction of the oil and the calculation of the net revenues, and the amounts for the relevant levels of government; the undermining of "our hard won peace" by foreign elements in Equatoria (the Lord's Resistance Army [LRA]) and Sudanese armed groups in other parts of the South and Southern Kordofan, for which the SAF and other government security organs were suspected by the public in South Sudan and Southern Kordofan of providing support; interference by some ministers and officials in GoNU who were establishing direct contacts with the South Sudan state governments, contrary to the CPA provisions that the GoNU could only access the state governments in the South through the GoSS; the failure to repeal or amend statutes and laws to comply with the INC of 2005 and the CPA, as "we cannot continue to be governed by laws that are in contravention of our own constitution"; and the delay in the process of restructuring the national civil service to make it more representative and professional. Salva Kiir ended the list by stating emphatically, "Unless we make progress on these matters, I cannot see how the rest of the CPA can survive."

Precariously poised between pursuing the vision of a New United Sudan and carefully buying time toward self-determination, the SPLM had to maintain a delicate balance in its uneasy partnership with the NCP. It had to press for reforms toward the vision of a New Sudan, if only in the long-term interest of its Northern allies, but it could not push too hard and risk a reaction that might threaten the collapse of the CPA and Southern self-determination. In this delicate equation, Garang's vision for a New Sudan receded after his death. In my discussion with Vice President Ali Osman Mohamed Taha, he argued, quite convincingly, that as they did not want to give labels to the system they had negotiated in the CPA, people should not dwell on what is meant by the concept of New Sudan, but should instead focus on a credible implementation of the CPA. To the extent that the Sudanese people will be content with the outcome, it would not matter what the resulting system is called.

Initially hailed for ending a war that had raged intermittently for half a century, and expected to generate a process of transformation in the country toward a New Sudan of nondiscrimination and equality for all, the CPA had paradoxically turned into a tool for the NCP containment of the South and the country as a whole. With the sudden and untimely death of Garang, the SPLM/A largely retreated to the South to consolidate the GoSS and await the end of the six-year interim period, when it expected the South to vote for full independence. The NCP appeared comfortable with that prospect. In a press interview in November 2006, President al-Bashir went as far as confessing that should the South choose to secede, the NCP would be the first to offer its congratulations. It was reported to me that the president further explained that this would enable the NCP to remain in power in the North. Even the 2009 midterm elections, which were supposed to provide the opportunity for alternative political alignments that might transform the country toward the New Sudan, seemed to offer no prospects for change, as the parties to the CPA preferred to maintain the status quo. There was even talk that they might decide to delay the elections. For the SPLM/A, any outcome that would unseat the NCP would mean bringing back to power the traditional political parties whose record on the South had been one of dismal failure and who were opposed to the CPA and, by implication, to the right of self-determination. In contrast, the NCP, though by no means trustworthy, was at least a partner in the CPA and the GoNU.

Despite persistent violations of the CPA, the parties appeared intent on avoiding a return to war. And, indeed, neither party was likely to gain from the resumption of hostilities. The South was exhausted after half a century of warfare, with aging veterans and a younger generation with an untested determination to fight. In contrast, the NCP had been strengthened by oil wealth, most of which was ironically from the South. On the other hand, any resumption of armed confrontation with the South was likely to rekindle the fires of war in the marginalized regions of the North. The convergence of those regional rebellions was most likely to overwhelm the center and the Arab Islamic domination of the country.

It must, however, be emphasized that while the positions presented above were broadly representative of the thinking in the NCP and the SPLM/A, there were dissenting views in both camps. With respect to the NCP, there were forces, by no means insignificant, that considered the CPA a bad deal for the North, and they would be inclined to find a way out of it. In the South, on the other hand, there were those who believed in preserving the NCP-SPLM partnership, while others wanted the SPLM to enter into alliances with political forces in the North to unseat the NCP, or at least form a sizeable opposition that could effectively check the NCP agenda for the country.

The meeting of the SPLM Interim National Council, held in Yei on February 8–12, 2007—the first since the death of Dr. John Garang—seemed to be a turning point. It not only reaffirmed the objectives of the movement, but also adopted a strategy for pursuing it nationally. This was, however, only a starting point, and there was no reason to expect the NCP to be complacent to the inherent threat to its dominance. Critical questions remained to be answered about the ambivalent partnership between the NCP and the SPLM/A, its implications for the midterm elections, and the precarious future of the border areas of Abyei, Southern Kordofan, and Blue Nile.

It is indeed worth remembering that the proliferating regional conflicts in Sudan are interconnected, and it would be a mistake to see any of them in isolation from developments in the rest of the country. Both in terms of root causes of the conflicts and the government response to the humanitarian consequences, these conflicts have much in common. Ultimately, a peace agreement that addresses the underlying cause of racial, regional, and cultural marginalization, even of the Islamic regions of the North, is the solution. To the extent that the Arab Islamic policy agenda cannot, in the long run, hold the country together, the goal must be to reverse this trend to provide a framework that accommodates all races, ethnicities, religions, cultures, and genders on equal footing. This remains valid even with the independence of the South.

## Attending Major Events in Sudan

The major events that I attended were central to Sudan's historical moment, poised as it was at a critical juncture between war and peace, unity and fragmentation, with both themes intertwined. Peace was successfully negotiated between the GoS and the SPLM/A, with considerable pressure from the international community, in particular the United

States. The goal of unity in a New Sudan was largely the vision of Dr. John Garang, initially mistrusted by the mainstream opinion in both the South and the North. With the passage of time, it became gradually accepted, especially by the marginalized groups and liberal elements in the North, and by increasing numbers in the South. The historic manner in which Garang was received in Khartoum, by multitudes estimated in the millions (Garang himself estimated six million), was testimony to the way he had inspired the nation across the North-South divide with his vision of a new, united but restructured Sudan. Had he lived, there is little doubt that he would have been the first South Sudanese president of the country.

His powerful vision was, however, confronted with the entrenched vision of the Old Sudan, which became even more strongly asserted the more it was threatened. This was evident at all critical junctures of the peace process: during the ceremonies of the signing of the CPA, at the swearing-in ceremony of Garang as first vice president, and in the immediate aftermath of his tragic death.

## The Signing of the CPA

I attended the signing of the CPA on January 9, 2005, at Nyayo Stadium, which was filled to capacity with Sudanese, Kenyans, and international observers. During the signing ceremonies, the conflicting identities were strongly reflected in the different forms of dress and dance by the respective groups from the North and the South. One prominent aspect of the confrontation was the alternation between chants of "*Allahu Akbar*" ("God is great") by an overzealous Muslim (ironically a Southerner, as I learned later) through a loudspeaker and recitations of the chorus of "Alleluia" by the Southern crowds in response. Another was the effect of the SPLA martial music, which evoked a spontaneous outburst from the Southern crowd, who sang the war songs of the SPLA. The lyrics of one of the songs evoked by the music was, "Our battalion knows no mercy; even my father, I will give him a bullet," about which President al-Bashir had complained to me as a perversion of Sudanese values. Prominent also was the jubilation of Southerners and the contrasting solemn mood of their Northern compatriots. Equally pronounced was the contrast between the conciliatory tone of the speeches of President al-Bashir and Vice President Ali Osman Taha and the long, matter-of-fact speech of Dr. John Garang, which restated in no uncertain terms what the war had all been about and how the CPA addressed those underlying causes. All in all, it was obvious that despite the jubilation over the agreement, there were lingering tensions that underscored the profundity of the conflicting visions for the country.

## Swearing-In Ceremony

I returned to Nairobi on July 5, 2005, and on July 7, I accompanied the SPLM/A leadership on their historic return to Khartoum, where I remained until July 21, witnessing the momentous return of Dr. John Garang de Mabior on July 8, and his swearing in as the first vice president of Sudan and president of the government of South Sudan on July 9. The return of John Garang and the massive reception with which he was honored by millions in the so-called green belt must have sent frightening signals to his Northern foes, who had become ambivalent partners. Sudan had never witnessed such support for a national leader from anywhere in Sudan in recent history. Garang's message in his statement at the swearing-in ceremony took advantage of that massive support. "You are now free," he told the Sudanese people. "Spread your wings and fly to even greater heights of freedom." But from whom were they free? I posed the question to Garang that evening, and he gave the answer: obviously from his former enemies, now allies in government, sitting next to him. He conceded to me that although armed struggle had ended, the conflict would continue in other forms.

In the swearing-in ceremony, Garang also announced that he planned to have the SPLM open offices all over the country, meaning that he was going to penetrate into the North to promote the vision of the New Sudan. I also questioned Garang on this strategy and what it would mean to his Northern foes/allies. As I pointed out to Garang, his plan was obviously to invade the constituencies that Northern leaders had always taken for granted and assumed to be outside the reach of Southern, non-Arab and non-Muslim leaders, whose vision and sphere of influence were expected to be limited only to the South. How would his peace partners and competitors by other means respond to that? I asked. Garang's response was, "I softened it by saying that it was one way to promote national unity."

At the swearing-in ceremony, once again, Garang reiterated the root causes of the war, which centered on the crisis of national identity and the imposition of a minority Arab Islamic identity on the majority of the Sudanese people, including in the North, where the majority were Muslims, but not Arab. He also restated his vision of the New Sudan, in which all citizens would be equal, without discrimination on the grounds of race, ethnicity, religion, culture, or gender.

Judging from these themes in Garang's statement to the nation, it was obvious that the partnership resulting from the CPA was an ambivalent coming together of visions for the country that represented polar extremes. When I asked Garang how he thought such an ambivalent partnership would work in practice, he admitted that it would not be easy and reiterated that, despite the peace agreement, the conflict would continue, albeit nonviolently. Garang restated a view he had often shared with me, that the mistake Southerners made with the 1972 Addis Ababa Agreement was to take it as the end to the conflict. He did not want the CPA to be viewed in the same vein. For him, the CPA was not an end in itself, but a phase in the ongoing process of transforming the country. Garang was fully aware that he posed a threat to the Arab Islamic establishment, but he saw that as the very reason he had taken up arms in the first place, and he was prepared to continue the struggle by other means.

Since his vision was national and not only Southern, resolving the other conflicts in the North was central to his agenda. He wanted the SPLM/A to play an active role in addressing the crisis in Darfur, and even offered 10,000 SPLA soldiers to join a national protection force in Darfur. In addition, he wanted the SPLM to be actively involved in the Darfur peace talks. He intimated to me that he had told his NCP partners in the GoNU that the best way to promote the lifting of international sanctions against Sudan was to show evidence of reform and a change of policy in Darfur that would be convincing to the international community. He said he was prepared to advocate the lifting of sanctions, but he challenged his partners to facilitate his efforts with tangible reforms.

It was indeed the hope of many that the principles of the CPA would be extended to the North to bring peace to the conflicts in Darfur, the Beja region, and other Northern areas of active or potential conflicts to make the peace agreement truly comprehensive. A widely shared expectation was that Garang would play an active role in this process, which in turn was expected to enhance the prospects for national unity.

## The Death of Dr. John Garang

When John Garang met his tragic and most untimely death in a helicopter crash on July 30, 2005, only three weeks after assuming the offices of first vice president of Sudan and president of South Sudan, I returned promptly and arrived in time to accompany his body with his family and the SPLM/A leadership through several towns, ending with his state burial in Juba. The public reaction to the death of John Garang was a most moving event to witness, with sharply contrasting cultural expressions. Among the Dinka, people do not cry over the death of a hero or a leader. Accordingly, when the body of John Garang arrived in the Dinka towns, Rumbek and Bor, the large crowds that received him, virtually all the inhabitants of those towns, were characterized by absolute silence, except for when the master of ceremonies used a loudspeaker for announcements. Occasionally, a woman would wail, but she was swiftly taken away. The absolute silence of such large crowds was most extraordinary.

In contrast, in the non-Dinka areas in Kauda, the Nuba Mountains, Yei, and Juba, the air was filled with wailing, not only by women, but also by men. The people in the crowds that lined the streets on both sides from the airport into town all seemed to be deafeningly crying. Some women threw themselves down to the ground or fainted. The sharp contrast with the Dinka response was stunning. And yet, in their different ways, it was so obvious that they felt orphaned and deeply aggrieved by the death of their hero and the father of their nation.

In Khartoum and in a number of Southern towns, suspicion that Garang must have been assassinated by his enemies in the North provoked riots that led to the death of many on both sides. But, although violence was initiated by Southerners in Khartoum, they became the primary victims of Northern retaliation, by both police and civilians. The situation was eventually brought under control by the intervention of the leadership on both sides.

As I had already been on good terms with Garang's successor, Salva Kiir, I met with him during the funeral period. My advice to him was to create a positive situation out of the tragedy. It was well known that he disagreed with Garang's way of running the SPLM/A. The tragedy of Garang's death also offered Kiir the opportunity to correct what he objected to in Garang's style of leadership. It was also well known that Garang had opponents in the South who threatened to weaken the region with divisiveness. Kiir's well-known tendency toward consultation and inclusiveness promised to be a force for unification in the South. But I advised him that while he needed to attract Garang's opponents in the SPLM/A, he also needed to ensure that they came with a genuine intention to join the movement and not with divisive goals either to win Salva Kiir to their side or to pursue their own agendas within the movement.

After Garang's death, his vision for a New Sudan began to recede from the rhetoric of the leadership in both the South and the North. Unity became increasingly unattractive to the South for a variety of reasons, including the post-Garang violence in Khartoum and problems associated with the implementation of the CPA.

Nevertheless, the implementation of the CPA proceeded relatively well. The GoNU and the GoSS and their various organs and institutions were smoothly established, albeit with challenges.

## The CPA: A Laudable but Ambivalent Achievement

The fact that the CPA held through the transitional period and is still holding is a laudable accomplishment. However, the credibility of implementation continues to be very challenging, as important issues remain unresolved and may still have the potential to undermine peace in the long run. Certainly, there was no evidence that unity was being made attractive, and it might never have been the intention of the ruling partners to do so. It was well known that the principal objective of the South was to exercise the right of self-determination after the six-year interim period, with secession as the preferred option. While the position of the NCP was less certain, it was widely believed that the party continued to entrench itself, and although the independence of the South was manifestly not desirable, it would free the North to pursue its Arab Islamic agenda, without the South as an impediment or a complicating factor.

However, the challenge for Sudan was not only the North-South conflict, but the pervading feeling of marginalization among the predominantly non-Arab groups in the country, including in the North. The vision of a New Sudan, though originally propounded by the SPLM, inspired a wide following in the North that was unlikely to be suppressed, even with Southern independence.

African countries, and the international community at large, wanted Sudan to remain united, although the right of the South to secede could no longer be denied. Sudan was a country whose vast size and geopolitical location, as well as its plentiful agricultural, mineral, and oil resources, gave it a strategic regional and international importance. The international community played a vital role in mediating the CPA. It was still called upon to contribute to ensuring its credible implementation and help promote and support reforms toward a restructured New Sudan that would be favorable to consensual unity. Should the South opt for secession, it was still necessary to support the reform agenda in the North toward an African-Arab peace and reconciliation. That was the only way the country could effectively play a moderating role between sub-Saharan black Africa and the Arab Muslim North Africa, whose identity extends into the Middle East. That role had long been postulated for Sudan, but it had largely remained an unrealized aspiration. But should Sudan perform the needed restructuring of the system toward the postulated New Sudan, a new foundation would be put in place that could support some form of association between Sudan and South Sudan.

Experience with the process of CPA implementation indicates the dilemmas Sudan was and is still confronting. The CPA was intended by one of its architects not as an end in itself, but as a tool for the transformation of the governance system in the country. Such a transformation would naturally threaten its Northern partner to the CPA. The principal partners' visions for the country were incompatible and irreconcilable. But the partners needed each other to protect their vested interests and safeguard the CPA.

This might be workable if the sole objective of the SPLM was a secession that would allow the NCP to continue its Arab Islamic agenda unchallenged. But Southern secession was no longer seen as a foregone conclusion in view of the postulated vision of a New Sudan. It was also becoming evident that even the goal of a credible implementation of the self-determination provisions of the CPA might ultimately depend on the power equations at the center, the first manifestation of which was the midterm election. The question then was whether the SPLM should stand in alliance with the NCP, to maintain the status quo under their ambivalent partnership, or enter into alliances with other political forces in the North to start a process of transformation.

This raised two additional questions: 1) What kind of preelection alliances or pacts, if any, needed to be developed that might consider some kind of ongoing role for the NCP in a coalition government, if there was any hope to convince the NCP hardliners that the time for their monopoly of power was up? 2) With which Northern political forces could the SPLM enter into alliances?

The traditional political parties came with historical baggage that was Arab-Islamic and adverse to the interests of the South and other marginalized areas. Besides, they remained ambivalent and perhaps even hostile to the CPA. As for the movements in the marginalized areas of the North that should have much in common with the South, they were disorganized, insufficiently focused, and far from being effective in shaping a national agenda and gaining popular support across the regional divides.

All this shows that there was an urgent need for a national debate about the future of the country. Perhaps what was unknown was the extent to which the traditional parties and the regional movements could enter into an alliance that could effectively transcend the NCP agenda and pave the way for a democratic transformation toward the New Sudan. While that was an internal matter for the Sudanese, the international community could assist in ensuring the integrity of the process and the conduct of free and fair elections.

The turning point in this development was the policy direction charted during the February 2007 meeting of the SPLM Interim National Council in Yei, which reaffirmed the movement's vision of a united New Sudan and resolved to relocate the SPLM headquarters from Juba to Khartoum. While some viewed that with skepticism, a genuine debate was increasing among Southerners on the merits and demerits of secession and the possibility of a New Sudan as a credible alternative. The SPLM needed to develop self-confidence and design mechanisms and strategies for influencing developments toward a Sudan of justice and equality that patriotic Sudanese could not but support. Even if the South should vote for secession, which it was expected to do, that vision was one that would continue to be pursued by the victims of the ongoing marginalization and gross inequality in the old order, who would remain on the front line in the struggle for transformation. For this reason, strategic thinking needed to begin on options for a "mutually advantageous coexistence by future new states of Southern and Northern Sudan."

The fundamental question was whether the national crisis of identity in Sudan was leading toward the fragmentation and disintegration of the country, or toward a rethinking of the national destiny in favor of a new vision that would bring together all the peoples of Sudan in a framework of inclusive national self-identification, with the pride and dignity of belonging, on equal footing, without any discrimination on the grounds of race, ethnicity, religion, culture, or gender. That was the SPLM's stated vision of the New Sudan, and it remained the only prospect for making unity attractive to Southerners as they contemplated the exercise of their right of self-determination in the 2011 referendum. It was also the only way forward to ensure the entrenchment of a process of change that could transcend a decision for secession and solidify alliances between an independent South Sudan and political forces in the North committed to a New Sudan. Armed struggle played its role for half a century after independence. It was time for the democratic transformation to take over within the framework of the CPA. That was where international support needed to be focused to encourage credible, free, and fair midterm elections and the 2011 self-determination referendum, with the normative objective of making unity an attractive option, or accepting an independence vote with the prospect of peaceful and cooperative relations between the two Sudans.

# Chapter Four: Government of National Unity (GoNU)

The GoNU was both quantitatively and qualitatively dominated by the NCP. The impact of the SPLM was only superficially visible, which was not only an encouragement for separation, but could indeed endanger the CPA as the level of frustration, already evident, was reaching a crisis point. Measures needed to be taken to strengthen and encourage the SPLM to be a more credible partner in the GoNU, capable of contributing effectively and visibly to shaping and reforming the national agenda. At the same time, the NCP needed to be constructively engaged to have an incentive in reforming the system from within. As the transformation of the country toward a New Sudan, united or divided, seemed ultimately unpreventable, the wisest option for the NCP was to swim with the current, rather than against it. That challenge has continued even after the independence of the South, although the NCP appears to have entrenched the status quo.

Ironically, the NCP has been strengthened in the North by the independence of the South. But the vision of a New Sudan is no longer the prerogative of the SPLM/A, which is identified with the South; the vision is now associated with the SPLM/A-North, which, for obvious reasons, remains tenuously connected to the South.

If the CPA was meant to provide a framework for a solid partnership between the NCP and the SPLM in the GoNU, actual performance fell notably short of that goal. The parties engaged each other out of necessity and were doing the minimum required to preserve the peace. In a sense, they remained bound together by the complex and intertwined conflicts afflicting the country. And yet, the differences between the North and South became more pronounced, which eventually led to the independence of the South.

The civil war was essentially about two identities that represented and continue to represent diametrically opposed models: an Arab Islamic model in the North and a more African-oriented, pluralistic, secular model in the South. The CPA ended hostilities and established an arrangement that brought the two polar extremes into a partnership of necessity. This resulted in an ambivalent collaboration that was widely perceived as nothing more than a new framework within which the parties continued to pursue their divergent objectives. The prevailing view was that, despite the stipulated percentages for sharing power and the numerous committees and commissions designed to ensure consultation and collaboration, the NCP still maintained control over the GoNU and was reticent to implement the CPA in any way that would undermine its power. Perhaps unwittingly, the CPA that was not only to free the South, but also to reform the Sudanese national governance agenda to lay the foundation for equitable unity, reinforced the North-South division of the country, and gave the NCP a new lease to continue its Arab Islamic agenda for the North.

## The Presidency

The power of implementing the CPA appeared to lie predominantly with the presidency, which was supposed to be jointly managed by the NCP and the SPLM, but became dominated by the NCP and President al-Bashir, especially after the death of Dr. John Garang. Salva Kiir was known not to be interested in the vision of a New United Sudan. Considerable discretionary powers were reserved for the presidency by the various provisions of the CPA. That presidency became one of President Omar al-Bashir. The broader question was whether a country that was supposed to be moving toward democratic pluralism should be deferring key decisions to a presidency that comprised disunited partners and was therefore either incapacitated by disunity or dominated by one of the parties. It became increasingly apparent that the CPA negotiating parties never envisioned such deadlocks within the presidency and, as a result, had not established practical dispute resolution mechanisms beyond the consideration of the presidency.

When Garang was received in Khartoum by millions from all over the country, al-Bashir was reported to have remarked, "I will probably be the last Arab President for the country." Garang's death radically changed the prospects for al-Bashir and his prospective Arab successor. Anecdotal evidence indicates that some elements in the Northern leadership rejoiced at Garang's death, and one leading figure even declared, "*Allahu Akbar*" ("God is great"). A prominent Southern opponent of John Garang who was in alliance with the Northern leadership also described Garang's death as "divine intervention" in favor of the South.

## The Cabinet

According to the CPA, the national executive was to be apportioned according to specified percentages to the NCP, SPLM, and other Northern and Southern political forces. This was done, although the Umma Party (mainstream), led by former prime minister Sadiq al-Mahdi, and the Popular National Congress, led by Hassan al-Turabi, declined to join the GoNU.

While the numbers generally matched up with the distribution under the CPA, the effective power and influence that the SPLM and opposition parties held was by no means a credible counterbalance to the NCP. First, as part of efforts to accommodate other political forces, it was alleged that the NCP had been breaking up ministries, creating new ones, and reallocating ministerial powers to strengthen its position. Second, it was alleged that in most cases, where an SPLM member held a federal ministerial position, the NCP state minister, who would typically act as the second in the hierarchy, or even the undersecretary, who was a civil servant, essentially assumed the key functions in the ministry. Third, it was widely believed that some of the SPLM-designated ministers and presidential advisers largely began to espouse the NCP party line on critical issues.

During the negotiations surrounding the ministerial appointments, an informal agreement was reached between the parties that the SPLM would hold the Ministry of Energy and Mining, while the NCP would be given control over the Ministry of Finance and National Economy. The NCP later reneged on this agreement and took both ministries, a decision Salva Kiir grudgingly accepted. Vice President Ali Osman Mohamed Taha explained to me that the Energy and Mining portfolio was highly technical and that the minister holding the position was the best person qualified for the job. First Vice President Salva Kiir, on the other hand, told me that he was not persuaded by that argument and that he gave in because he did not consider going back to war over the issue an option.

To balance this loss, the SPLM expected to chair and control the National Petroleum Commission (NPC), on which the Southern states had the majority of members. The NCP, however, argued that the minister of energy and mining should chair that commission. That met with strong protest by the other members of the commission, who wanted it to be independent and separate from the Ministry of Energy and Mining. That impasse resulted in great delays and rendered the commission largely dysfunctional.

## The National Assembly

The Transitional National Assembly had 450 seats, of which 234 were held by the NCP, 126 by the SPLM, 55 by the Northern political forces, 27 by the non-SPLM Southern political forces, and 8 by nonparty national personalities. The SPLM claimed that the assembly did not operate in the spirit of the CPA or the envisaged partnership. They alleged that critical documents were not circulated in time and not provided in English. Moreover, controlling its agenda through its majority, the NCP managed to keep the assembly from reviewing and modifying the many existing laws that were likely to be incompatible with the Interim National Constitution and the CPA.

While these complaints were probably justified, there was also a capacity issue for the SPLM. There were certainly very capable SPLM members in the GoNU, although it was observed that the party's struggle to rebuild itself after Garang's death, the difficult efforts to transform itself from a liberation movement into a political party, the practice of appointing senior-ranking SPLM members over other qualified professionals, and the uncertainty in setting out clear priorities and work plans all took a toll on the party. Some argued that the problem was compounded by a lack of political will or inclination to confront the NCP on issues. On the other hand, Salva Kiir and his SPLM colleagues, both inside the country and abroad, complained publicly about the way the NCP was subverting the implementation of the CPA. Their overriding consideration, however, was to avoid taking any action that would risk the resumption of hostilities and jeopardize the Southern self-determination referendum.

It must be acknowledged that many SPLM members also had limited practical experience in administration and management of government institutions and processes. Even if formally well educated, they often lacked the expertise related to their ministerial responsibilities. This made the quest for parity more difficult, especially as the state machinery had been restructured and efficiently controlled by the NCP for over a decade and a half. I recall asking John Garang whether an independent South could employ expertise from abroad or whether Southerners would be too sensitive about that. John Garang did not hesitate in giving me a positive answer: He would have no problem with making use of foreign expertise. Some of this has occurred under Salva Kiir, but not to the extent of a critical mass.

## Commissions Formation, Functioning, and Effectiveness

The commissions, which took time to be established, included the Human Rights Commission and the Civil Service Commission (which was key to filling the percentage of positions in the national government allocated to the South by the CPA). Draft laws for each of these commissions had been prepared by the Ministry of Justice and sent for review to the National Constitutional Review Commission (NCRC). It was hoped that these laws would be finalized and adopted during the next session of the assembly beginning on October 30, 2006. While commendable efforts had been initiated by civil society to contribute to this process, much was left to be done to ensure transparency and public participation.

There were also reports that critical commissions were underfunded, such as the Technical Ad Hoc Border Committee, which was to demarcate the 1956 North-South borders. In spite of the importance of this committee to the issue of oil allocation, the census, the redeployment of forces, the Joint Integrated Units formation, the 2009 elections and referendum, and overall jurisdictional and peace issues, at the time of my visit in 2006–07, this body had only met six times and its members had only just visited Juba, but not the border areas.

Moreover, many argued that a number of the commissions already established by decree and functioning (to varying extents) required a legislative base to ensure compliance with the CPA and consensus regarding their mandate, scope, and authority. Those included the National Petroleum Commission and the Fiscal and Financial Allocation and Monitoring Commission (FFAMC).

## The Call for Law Reform

The reconstitution of the National Constitutional Review Commission and the commencement of its work were elements that argued for the glass being half full. As its various subcommittees and sixty members examined critical legislation, including the National Security Act, Political Parties Act, Political Parties Registration Act, Civil Service Commission Act, Human Rights Commission Act, and the National Electoral Law, close attention needed to be paid to two factors that could ensure a reform that was pivotal to the permanent transformation of governance in Sudan.

First, the CPA had created space for a revitalized civil society that had begun efforts to organize greater participation of opposition political parties, jurists, and NGOs in the law reform process. There were impediments, however, to making this participation effective. These included a lack of access to decision makers, the absence of established procedures in the NCRC for public input, a lack of transparency (e.g., the prior release of draft bills for public comment), the marginal participation of opposition parties, and a still-nascent culture of openness to public participation.

The second impediment to law reform at the national level was the SPLM's seeming lack of interest in the long-term reform of national laws, preferring to focus on the situation in the South. Participation at the national level was apparently perceived as futile, time consuming, and distracting from the primary objectives of the South. A senior SPLM authority stated categorically that the laws of the GoNU were primarily of concern to the North and not to the South. He argued that since *sharia*, or Islamic law, was recognized by the CPA as a source of legislation for the North, there was little the South could do to ensure the secularization of the legal system. This was the core of the contradictions of the CPA: giving the South the right to secede, stipulating unity as an objective to be pursued and made attractive to the South, and affirming the Arab Islamic agenda of the NCP for the North. The contradictions were further compounded by the fact that the CPA simultaneously affirmed numerous principles of democracy and human rights that conflicted with *sharia*. There were also a vast number of laws that had little to do with Islam, and would affect the country as a whole.

The national Ministry of Justice repeatedly stated—and the minister personally confirmed to me—that it was in the process of revising existing laws in order to conform with the CPA and the Interim National Constitution. However, no progress was visibly made in that direction. There was also, in fact, a general complaint from the legal profession that the public was not being informed about the laws that needed reform and the direction the reform would take.

There were also conflicting views from the South on the issue. The president of the GoSS, Salva Kiir, repeatedly called for the repeal or reform of laws that conflicted with the provisions of the CPA. On the other hand, on a number of occasions, the minister of legal affairs and constitutional development of the GoSS and other senior members of the ministry expressed a lack of interest in law reform at the national level, considering that to be the concern of the GoNU. It was difficult to see how Southerners could be indifferent to the laws of the country that must inevitably affect them as citizens, at least during the interim period. That lack of interest, however, also indicated a predisposition toward secession, which conflicted with the stipulation of striving to make unity attractive and the SPLM affirmation of the vision of a New United Sudan.

According to a senior South Sudanese judge in the GoNU, even if the South were intent on secession, it would require legal procedures to bring that about. Whether the referendum on self-determination would be held and how it would be conducted would depend on the law that would be adopted for the purpose—particularly the Southern Sudan Referendum Act. Even the definition of who qualified as a Southerner for the purpose of voting was likely to be controversial. In his view, all legislation relating to elections, census, voting, and the position of absentees in the North and abroad was likely to be determined by the North to the disadvantage of the South. The way the relevant laws would be formulated, in his view, would determine the outcome.

The controversy over the newly adopted political parties law (a necessary step for free, fair, and transparent elections) was indicative of the stakes involved. The law was adopted at the end of January 2007, and prompted the withdrawal from the GoNU of the members of the National Democratic Alliance, who opposed a language it deemed discriminatory to non-CPA political parties. Also controversial was the SPLM-initiated article 18.b that would allow a court to dissolve a political party if the party was found to have engaged in activities to "overthrow the constitutional system established under the provisions of the CPA and the INC."

## Involvement of Opposition Parties

It was widely recognized that the CPA could not truly transform Sudan as long as only two parties controlled its implementation. While there might have been good reasons for limiting the number of parties in the peace negotiations, given the electoral strength of the traditional parties repeatedly demonstrated in the past, they had understandable grievances against the CPA's bilateral power arrangements. The real question was whether these parties would have a chance to increase their power in the 2009 national elections. This would depend on the extent to which the elections were free and fair. The consensus was that, unless significant steps were immediately taken to ensure that they would be transparently free and fair, the NCP's political machinery, superior access to financial resources, and state control would almost certainly cause it to be favored over the other parties. However, given the past failures of the traditional parties to resolve the pressing problems of the country, including the war in the South, it was not easy to predict how they would fare, even in free and fair elections. Nevertheless, the devoted support of their followers was still an important consideration in their favor. These proportional advantages and disadvantages have continued to characterize the relative positions of the NCP and the traditional parties in the power dynamics of Sudan.

## The NCP Point of View

The NCP, which often took the brunt of the blame for lack of progress in the implementation of the CPA, explained away or justified the situation by citing practical difficulties and operational constraints or placing the blame on the SPLM/A. The official position of the party was forcefully stated by President Omar al-Bashir during his November 2006 address to the joint meeting of the South Sudan cabinet and the Legislative Assembly in Juba. Responding to the complaints of the South about the slow implementation of the CPA, the president gave as reasons the delayed return of the SPLM leadership to Khartoum following the signing of the CPA, the tragic death of John Garang and its impact, and the preparation of appropriate legislation for the establishment of commissions and other institutions stipulated in the CPA. The president sounded quite genuine when he declared that his party sincerely hoped that the South would vote for unity, but should the result come out in favor of independence, they hoped South Sudan and North Sudan would be the best of neighbors. This was the first statement by a Northern leader that envisioned relations between the North and the South in the event of Southern independence. It was no wonder that this part of the president's statement received the loudest applause.

The president's sentiment was repeated to me by leading members of the NCP, although it was nearly always combined with sharp criticism of the attitude of the SPLM/A partners in the GoNU. A senior NCP official put it bluntly: "Frankly, we do not feel that our partner is as reliable as we had hoped." In particular, NCP leaders were critical of the tendency of the first vice president and president of the GoSS, Salva Kiir, and other members of the SPLM to air their differences publicly, which they contrasted with the attitude of President al-Bashir, whom they argued never publicly criticized Salva Kiir or discussed in public the differences between the GoNU partners. With a degree of condescension, senior members of the NCP attributed what they saw as the weaknesses of the SPLM and the GoSS to a lack of expertise and experience, having been fighters in the jungle for decades. One senior member of the NCP said that the president felt like an elder brother who must be patient with the behavior of his younger brothers in the South.

Although the NCP leadership claimed that the party stood united in its commitment to the CPA and acceptance of any decision the South would make in the referendum, it was also known that there were strong critics of the CPA who wanted a pretext to repudiate it. The view, first voiced by the secretary-general of the NCP, Dr. Ibrahim Ahmed Omer, that the NCP would pull out of the CPA if the UN forces intervened in Darfur without the consent of the government and the SPLM/A continued to support such intervention, was apparently widely shared within the party.

## The Southern Point of View

Southerners generally remained convinced that the NCP was hostile to the CPA and was looking for ways of undermining it and eventually extricating itself from it. Perhaps the most immediate indicator of this was the alleged continuous use of militias and other armed groups to create insecurity in the South and destabilize the GoSS. This was a concern that was highlighted by the chairman of the CPA's Assessment and

Evaluation Commission (AEC). Calling the continued presence of militias a "serious violation of the CPA," the Norwegian chairman Tom Vraalsen stated that, "at this stage, two years after the signing of CPA, there is no room for militias in the South."

Although those groups were sometimes said to be remnants of militias that had refused to join the SPLA or be integrated into the Sudan Armed Forces in the North, they allegedly continued to be supported by the Sudan Army. While there had been a series of incidents in and around Juba and other areas of the South, perhaps the most serious was the November 18–29, 2006, incident in Malakal, where the SAF forces openly backed Southern militias under Gabriel Tang and Mabor Dhol in a confrontation with the SPLA. To protect him, the SAF lifted Tang by helicopter to Khartoum. The incident was serious enough to force President Salva Kiir to interrupt an official visit to South Africa, return to the South, and press on to Malakal. In the aftermath of this incident, President Salva Kiir and the SPLM secretary-general directly accused the NCP of supporting Southern militias. In addition to these incidents in the South, a series of incidents involving SPLA forces in the Joint Integrated Units and the Khartoum police not only resulted in deaths on both sides, but created a situation in which the police reportedly patrolled and harassed South Sudanese neighborhoods, causing much concern about the security of Southerners in the capitol city.

While those proliferating violent incidents were contained, they raised the question of whether their containment indicated that the CPA was holding and successfully managing any potential crises, or descending into a gradual resumption of large-scale hostilities. On the conscious level, neither party wanted to go back to war, but deep-seated animosity and mistrust still provided fertile grounds for a potential breach of the agreement, with unintended consequences that could conceivably lead to a resumption of hostilities. During his visit to Juba in November 2006, President al-Bashir urged the Southerners not to take incidents by individuals in the SAF as indication of official support for those incidents, but to take them for what they were—isolated actions. He, however, pledged to end the activities of the militias in the South by January 2007—which, perhaps inadvertently, indicated some connection with SAF.

Southerners generally believed that the NCP was not intent on honoring the self-determination referendum and that they would either find a pretext for not allowing it or would declare an independence vote as null and void on some contrived grounds. The validity of this fear was to be tested by the NCP-controlled National Legislature in discharge of its constitutional obligation to draft and adopt the Southern Sudan Referendum Act. It was that act that would authorize the presidency to establish the Southern Sudan Referendum Commission, which would organize the referendum "in cooperation" with the national government and the GoSS. Delays in the adoption of the act, as well as the nature of the law itself, could be used to control the referendum process and outcome.

Whether the South would eventually secede or remain in a united Sudan, what was already obvious to Southerners was that the NCP continued to engage actively in the classic Northern strategy of dividing the South to weaken it and ensure its continued domination. This was done by encouraging factionalism among Southern political forces, particularly ambitious non-SPLM Southern leaders who were opposed to the SPLM/A, and by co-opting SPLM ministers in the GoNU. Despite public disagreements with the policies and actions of the NCP, the party appeared to be running the show, and it was quite successful in turning the CPA into a tool for containment of the South and the other marginalized regions. There was hardly any challenge to the NCP, except for the critical reactions of a few voices from the SPLM, which were mostly dismissed as a rhetorical nuisance, without practical consequences.

## Northern Opposition Point of View

The result of these dynamics was that the CPA, which was meant to be a means of transforming the system of rule in the country and mobilizing political forces across the board toward that goal, paradoxically entrenched the status quo and the dominance of the NCP. Ironically, the Northern opposition parties—particularly the Popular National Congress Party and the Umma Party—continued to look on the SPLM/A as the only force that could alter the balance of power in favor of a major political reform in the country. Perhaps with some wishful thinking, they saw the NCP as having failed in its grand Islamic design, becoming politically bankrupt, running out of ideas, and heading for doom. One prominent leader of the opposition told me that the NCP was 80 percent gone, holding to only 20 percent, and at its eleventh hour.

The problem those opposition parties faced in winning alignment with the SPLM/A was not only their historical baggage, which was one of unmitigated failure for the South, but also their ambivalence on the CPA, which typically manifested itself as opposition. While they were willing to honor the provisions relating to the South, they disapproved of the unqualified international reverence for the CPA as a "holy cow." They considered the CPA an untenable agreement between two parties to the exclusion of a wide array of more representative political forces. This confronted the SPLM with a serious dilemma. On the one hand, the leadership and the base recognized that the Arab Islamist ideology and political agenda of the NCP made them an odd couple. On the other hand, the NCP was their partner in the CPA and it had committed itself to the provision most important to the South, the right of self-determination. Since what was of pivotal value to the South was the right to secede rather than making unity attractive, the SPLM partnership with the NCP was the most promising, and therefore it was worth preserving. That strategy could even inform how strongly the SPLM engaged on law reform relevant to ensuring free and fair elections. Opposition parties were already expressing fear that the new Political Parties Act that was approved by the National Assembly Legislation and Justice Committee would be used to suppress the political opposition.

While the view of maintaining the status quo in the North was allegedly shared by President Salva Kiir, not all the members of the SPLM, even at the higher levels, agreed with this position. The alternative perspective, which the late Dr. John Garang would have espoused, was that the CPA was not an end in itself, but a tool for transforming the country toward the vision of the New Sudan. As such, alliances with other political forces in the North, especially from the marginalized regions, would be a tactically strategic move toward that objective. Those people argued, as Garang would have done and had indeed done, that even if the goals of the South were regional, influencing the power equations at the center was essential to ensuring those goals. Those competing visions, which divided even the top leadership, presented the South with a serious challenge.

An interesting development that seemed to indicate that the NCP and the SPLM might, paradoxically, be growing closer, albeit with continuing ambivalence, was the visit of Sudan's president to Juba in November 2006. The warm reception he got from the GoSS; the lavish praise he received from the Southern leaders, including President Salva Kiir; and President al-Bashir's enthusiastic and seemingly sincere commitment to the credible implementation of the CPA (the case of the Abyei Protocol being a glaring exception) were all notable. In his statement, Salva Kiir praised al-Bashir as "a courageous, brave, and firm son of the Sudan, who truly stands for the unity of the country." In another context, Salva Kiir said, "The people of the Sudan in general and Southerners in particular, are very grateful and thankful for the courageous and brave step that the Government of Sudan, led by the National Congress Party, under your able wise leadership[,] and the SPLM/A, under the then wise leadership of our late hero, Dr. John Garang de Mabior, God rest his soul in peace, were brave enough to conclude and sign the long awaited peace, which our people have suffered long enough to achieve." Salva Kiir went on to say, "The trust and confidence that the people of Sudan in general and Southerners in particular have placed upon your unprecedented leadership, have no doubt created an atmosphere of patience and hope that the CPA is on its rightful track towards its final implementation." Since the full confidence and admiration reflected in those words of exaltation were widely recognized as incongruent with the adversarial relations that had prevailed, their only significance was that they offered an incentive for the NCP leader to rise to the envisioned role for which he was being preemptively praised. President al-Bashir's visit to Juba in celebration of the second anniversary of the CPA was far less conciliatory, and a tough exchange of blame between Salva Kiir and the president was widely reported.

In response to a complaint from the SPLM leadership about the lack of contact and cooperation between the ministers in the GoSS and their counterparts in the GoNU, President al-Bashir proposed an annual meeting in Khartoum between the two cabinets and between the respective ministers individually to share their programs and projects and explore ways in which the GoNU could provide support for their colleagues in the GoSS. Although this was a positive response to Southern complaint, it could foster an attitude of dependency of Southern ministers on their Northern counterparts in the GoNU for support, and could have the unintended consequence of fostering subordination and reinforcing the pattern of containment.

What all this indicated was that momentum for a degree of effective implementation of the CPA was building up, although some contradictory trends reflected the situation's precariousness and cautioned against complacency. The delicate balance between cautious optimism and pessimistic realism was reflected in the mixed responses to the question as to whether the CPA's glass was still half-empty or becoming half-full.

## Demarcation of the North-South Borders

Demarcation of the 1956 North-South borders was of great interest to the parties as it would determine vital issues such as the distribution of oil revenues, troop redeployment, the census results, and national budget allocation. The Technical Ad Hoc Border Committee established to demarcate the North-South borders was initially impeded in its work by lack of funds. Although funds were eventually allocated, it was still alleged that inadequate support for the transport and accommodation of the committee's Southern members to attend meetings in Khartoum significantly constrained their effective participation.

It was reported in January 2007 that the committee had completed its preliminary review of maps and had began a series of trips to the states bordering the 1956 line to inform the communities of its work and collect data. It was expected that the committee would conduct trips to the United Kingdom and Egypt to review maps there before finalizing its recommendations and submitting them to the presidency by October 2007.

Additionally, the impasse on the Abyei Boundary Commission's report, which was widely acknowledged as oil related, offered some indication of how the North-South border determination would likely play out. In a meeting at the United States Institute of Peace (USIP) in Washington, D.C., a senior member of the NCP candidly predicted that, should the South decide to secede, the contest over the oil fields in the border areas was likely to generate conflict. The secession of the South would not be a peaceful one, he said emphatically.

## The Distribution of Oil Revenues

One of the most contentious issues between the two parties was the distribution of oil revenues. While the National Petroleum Commission was intended to act as a controlling authority on the Ministry of Energy and Mining, the ministry continued to negotiate and sign new contracts without full disclosure or the approval of the commission. The areas of concern regarding the management of the oil sector were numerous, but mainly involved the failure to operationalize the institutions for the transparent oversight of the contracts with oil companies; the social and environmental problems associated with oil production, monitoring production, marketing, and accruing revenues; and the distribution of the revenues in accordance with the CPA allocations.

While the NCP insisted that South Sudan was receiving its allocated shares of the oil revenues, the general perception in the South was that Khartoum was shortchanging the GoSS, especially as information on the production, marketing, and revenue generation was not transparently made available. Later, after independence, this would eventually lead the GoSS to conclude that Sudan was "stealing" the oil, prompting South Sudan to shut down oil production, a measure that necessitated the introduction of austerity measures, severely aggravated the tensions between the two on the management of the oil sector, and was universally condemned by the international community. Khartoum retaliated by threatening to stop South Sudan's oil from flowing through the Northern pipeline. It was the intense mediation by the regional and international community that eventually ended the crisis.

## Security Concerns and Setbacks

By far the most critical area of the CPA was that of security arrangements. Among the security institutions and mechanisms that were
critical to the CPA were the Ceasefire Political Commission (CPC),
the Area Joint Military Committee (AJMC), and the Joint Defense Board
(JDB). Those were the mechanisms responsible for the supervision, verification, and monitoring of progress on troop redeployment, formation, training, and armament. It was alleged by the SPLM that the efforts
of the CPC were being frustrated by the failure of the presidency (meaning President al-Bashir) to make decisions on matters referred to it.

The Other Armed Groups Collaborative Committee (OAGCC) was
a mechanism for ascertaining the strength and armament of all the
OAGs, supervising and reviewing their incorporation into the forces of
the two CPA parties and monitoring the disarmament, demobilization,
and reintegration (DDR) program. As late as 2007, it was reported that
this body had not been meeting regularly and that not much had been
done to ensure timely implementation of the provisions on OAGs. An
area of particular concern was the continued presence of the OAGs, the
PDF, and paramilitary formations beyond the dates specified in the security arrangements. While the formation and organization of the Joint
Integrated Units had progressed relatively well, except in the three border
areas, the provisions of the security arrangements relating to uniformity
in training, doctrine, and armaments for the JIUs had not been implemented. It was also alleged that, "contrary to the provisions of the Security Arrangements, the Sudan Armed Forces (SAF) was behind schedule
in redeploying its troops outside Southern Sudan and, contrary to the
CPA, was resisting force reduction in the three transitional areas, and
was in fact increasing its forces in the oil-fields in greater Upper Nile and
the Three Areas."

A major factor in the tenuous security situation in the South was the
failure to absorb the tribal militias into either the SAF or the SPLA.
The SAF claimed that 7,407 of its soldiers, who were still in Juba, Wau,
and Malakal, had refused to be redeployed to the North, and it was
pensioning them off. It was reported, however, that they were still in

their barracks, receiving their salaries, and fully armed. Those situations produced widespread insecurity in the South, involving a series of violent incidents and massacres in various areas. While the GoSS authorities, including President Salva Kiir, repeated substantiated allegations of continuing SAF support for militias in the South, the NCP flatly denied this. In his statement in Juba on January 9, 2007, President al-Bashir stated categorically, "As Commander-in-Chief, I am telling you—we have no relations with militias." At the same time, however, he admitted that "30,000 of the 40,000 militiamen active in the South had been disarmed but the job could not be finished overnight."

Allegations were made that the forces withdrawn from the South or set for redeployment had been moved to the border areas of Abyei, Southern Kordofan, Blue Nile, the oil-rich area of Bentiu, and the Copper Valley (Hofrat El-Nahas) in Bahr El Ghazal. In Abyei, the buildup was of particular concern, given the ban imposed by both parties that prevented the UN verification and monitoring forces from moving north or south of Abyei Town. The continued support by the NCP of other armed groups and militias added to the precariousness of peace.

One UN official told me that the SAF did not even try to hide its support of militias. There were cases where militias had been caught, turned over to the UN, and then when the SAF was approached with the arrests, it outright admitted that they were their men, though not formally absorbed into the SAF as required by the CPA. The attacks by armed forces in the outskirts of Juba that killed about forty people, though initially thought to be perpetrated by the Ugandan Lord's Resistance Army, were now reportedly attributed to disgruntled members of Southern militias that were aligned to the SAF but had not been integrated into either the government forces in the North or the SPLA. When the government stopped paying them—a decision later reversed—they became embittered and prone to banditry. The attacks were assumed to be part of a pattern that was aggravating the security situation in Equatoria and specifically around Juba.

There was a growing fear that those armed elements would continue to be used by the NCP to destabilize the South and undermine the realization of free and fair elections in 2009 and the self-determination referendum in 2011. Even then, it had become obvious to serious observers that the South was heading for secession. Yet, there was wishful thinking in the North that, by hook or by crook, the country would be kept united.

## Efforts to Divide the South and Undermine the SPLM

Ironically, the way to promote unity from the perspective of the North was to create disunity in the South. This was pursued not only by continuing support for the armed groups that had resisted joining the SPLA without being absorbed by the SAF, but also by striving to co-opt SPLM ministers in the GoNU, not to join the NCP, but to support its policies against the position of their own party. It should be emphasized that only a few were often identified as following the NCP policy lines. This matter was seriously discussed in the SPLM Political Bureau meetings that were held in Juba on September 14 and 16, 2007. In addition to placing blame on individuals, it was admitted that the SPLM had not been sufficiently engaged on national issues, and it was reportedly agreed that the ministers in the GoNU should maintain close contact among themselves and with their colleagues in the GoSS and that periodic strategic meetings should be held to clarify and disseminate the SPLM position on critical national issues. Some SPLM members in the GoNU were in fact quite combatant in their staunch stand for their party's principles and policies.

Those SPLM members who were resisting co-optation tended to be undermined and isolated in a variety of ways. Already known were the allegations that prior to the formation of the GoNU, the powers of certain ministries were redistributed to weaken those ministries allocated to the SPLM. As noted earlier, NCP ministers of state and undersecretaries regularly undermined SPLM ministers. In fact, it was reported that in NCP-controlled ministries, there were cases where a senior minister would travel unbeknownst to his SPLM state minister, who would normally act as the minister in charge. The effective control and management of the ministry then passed down to the undersecretary. This tactic of undermining SPLM power had even extended to the Southern state level. There were reports that GoNU officials often bypassed the GoSS and engaged directly with the local governments and governors of the Southern states (particularly in areas related to oil production and potential contracts). This was a violation of the CPA division of powers, which provided that "the linkage between the National Government and the states in the Southern Sudan shall be through the Government of Southern Sudan."

Yet another instance of Southerners being used to divide the South included those members of the GoNU who represented other political parties that opposed the SPLM and tended to align themselves with the NCP. While their long-term objectives might have been to serve the interest of the South as they saw it, by cooperating with Northern adversaries for positions of power or material gains, they wittingly or unwittingly hurt Southern interests.

In this complex situation of cross-purpose alignments and counterproductive political maneuvers, Southerners still retained the belief that something more fundamental united them and that they should not give up any fellow Southerners as irretrievably "lost." The aspiration on both sides was to find ways of generating dialogue with a view to promoting consensus and unity of purpose. This was particularly true of Southerners who were cooperating with the NCP and who realized their vulnerability to allegations of having betrayed the cause of their people. But their pride or the lure of power and wealth inhibited them from stooping for acceptance. This called for some thoughtful, face-saving moves from the GoSS, specifically from President Salva Kiir.

In addition, although all of the state constitutions had been adopted in the South, in late September 2006, the GoNU minister of justice refused to certify the constitutions as being in conformity with the Interim National Constitution (ostensibly because the constitutions identified state capitals and jurisdictional boundaries).

The question of whether the country was headed toward consolidating unity or toward partition was most pronounced during the interim period and in the so-called Government of National Unity, which in effect was a Government of National Disunity.

## SPLM: Rising to the Occasion?

It was observed that too often the SPLM members in the GoNU did not keep their Southern counterparts abreast of critical developments and policy formations occurring at the center. This lack of communication had also been witnessed in various commissions where SPLM participants were reported to have less than consistent attendance and often failed to report back to their members about developments and outstanding debates. This weakened the party's ability to offer strong, unified, and consistent policies and positions at the national level and contributed to a perception of Southern detachment from the national agenda. Largely due to a dearth of qualified individuals, the SPLM assigned multiple critical posts to a number of people. For instance, one Southern parliamentarian, based in Juba, also served on the NCRC, which met in Khartoum. Another crucial SPLM member of the NCRC also had a lead role in the GoSS assembly's robust legislative agenda. Those multiple assignments often undermined the attention that a given issue required. Additionally, it was said that First Vice President Salva Kiir was somewhat withdrawn from the GoNU, often reacting to situations in which President al-Bashir and the NCP took the lead, rather than affirmatively pushing the limits of his authority as a member of the collegiate presidency. Kiir's main interest was to mark time for the Southern Referendum and ensure the independence of the South.

## The Prospects for Transformation

The remarkable thing about the CPA was that it was premised on two apparently contradictory but in fact complementary principles: the right of the South to internal self-determination and the obligation of the parties to make unity an attractive option in the exercise of that right. The contradiction was implicit in the fact that the South, it was generally predicted, would opt for secession, while the unity of the country, it was also generally agreed, was the preferred option. Could the two be reconciled? That was a question for which there was no easy answer, but the premise was that they were indeed reconcilable.

There were conflicting perspectives among both Northerners and Southerners on the issue. From the Northern perspective, there were those who saw the South as a liability and would be happy to see it go. In fact, some went as far as demanding the right of secession for the North. On the other hand, there were Northerners, presumably the majority, who wanted Sudan to remain united. However, available evidence indicated that this group was not prepared to make unity attractive to the South by radically transforming the system of governance to remove the discrimination and domination based on the Arab Islamic framework represented by the NCP. Containing the South and other marginalized non-Arab regions in the North therefore appeared to be the essence of the compromises in the peace agreements they were willing to conclude with these regions.

In the South, on the other hand, while the overwhelming aspiration was for Southern independence, and Garang's vision of a New Sudan was accepted by Southerners only as a ploy to allay the concerns against secession in Africa and internationally, the degree to which that vision had inspired the marginalized regions of the North and liberally minded Northerners began to have an impact on Southern perspectives. In particular, the position of the border areas of Southern Kordofan and Blue Nile, which, although still identified with the North, had become closely tied to the South, was increasingly becoming a significant factor in the potential outcome.

Paradoxically, developments indicated that the SPLM/A vision of a New Sudan was gaining ground among Southerners. In the Yei meeting of the Interim National Council in February 2007, the movement reaffirmed its commitment to the vision of a united New Sudan, decided to relocate its headquarters from Juba to Khartoum, and undertook to transform itself into a national party. This was confirmed by Angelina Riak Teny, wife of then vice president Riek Machar and SPLM state minister for energy and mining in the GoNU, who was widely reported to have announced at a conference of international investors in Nairobi in March 2007 that the South would vote for unity in the self-determination referendum. She was reported to have said, "As SPLM/A, we have decided that working for a united Sudan is the only way to stability." She elaborated at the Yei meeting of the Interim National Council: "We agreed that we will still need to work for stabilizing both the North and the South."

Although Angelina Riak Teny's statement generated controversy and might even have been taken out of context, it indicated a significant turn of events in the emerging debate on secession and unity. In a discussion with me, the minister said that while the SPLM should continue to cooperate with the NCP in the implementation of the CPA, it must reach out to other political forces in the North to work together for the transformation of the system toward the New Sudan that would make unity attractive.

As another SPLM minister in the GoNU explained, the diligence with which that policy would be pursued, and its prospects of success, would very much depend on the strength of the leadership and its commitment to the vision. As he put it, "leadership is elastic; when pulled, it will respond to the call, but when released, it will fall back."

## Impact of Developments on the NCP-SPLM Partnership

The developments outlined above were having a cumulative impact on the partnership between the NCP and the SPLM that was conspicuously ambivalent. While they publicly exchanged acrimonious allegations against each other's performance, they also realized that their cooperation was essential for the success of the CPA and their own survival. And yet, that success remained in jeopardy with the depth of suspicion and lack of confidence on both sides.

Southerners generally continued to believe that the NCP was not serious about implementing the CPA credibly. The North saw the CPA as an outside imposition that gave the South what it wanted by ensuring its full control of its own affairs and also giving it a significant say in the affairs of the country at the national level. While the NCP could not fully disengage from the CPA, its strategy was allegedly to weaken it in the process of implementation so that its impact on the overall national situation was minimized. And yet, it was believed that Vice President Ali

Osman Mohamed Taha and those NCP members who had been directly involved in negotiating the CPA were still committed to its good-faith implementation. According to one senior member of the party who had been involved in the negotiations, the core members of the NCP team that participated in the negotiations met weekly to assess the progress of implementation with a view to ensuring its credibility. But they were also said to be marginalized in the NCP, which made some of them become defensively more assertive of the party's hard line. It was also widely believed that Garang would have been a strong force behind the implementation of the CPA and the process of transformation toward the New Sudan. His tragic death at a crucial point removed that force and emboldened the NCP to pull back on its commitments.

A quick review of the functioning of some of the institutions of the GoNU underscores the SPLM complaints against the NCP. Perhaps the most outstanding discrepancy between what was stipulated in the CPA and what was in fact occurring related to the presidency. According to the agreement, the presidency was supposed to be collegial, which required close cooperation between the president (NCP) and the first vice president (SPLM). In practice, however, "many decisions were taken without the participation of the SPLM component of the Presidency." It was also alleged that "in most cases, the opinion of the SPLM in the Council of Ministers was presumed and not given weight as a full partner," which made "the SPLM have little or no influence in the running of the government."

In the legislature, there was generally more effective cooperation between the NCP and the SPLM. Nevertheless, it was alleged that the NCP sometimes tended to pass resolutions by relying on its "mechanical" majority rather than seeking consensus; that the SPLM was relegated to a marginal role in the administration of the legislature; that most bills were not translated into English, which would have allowed a more active participation of the Southern members in their consideration; and that there was a major difference between the legislative priorities of the NCP and those of the SPLM. The same picture was reflected in the functioning of the national commissions, the Population Census Council, the Technical Ad Hoc Border Committee, the national judiciary, and the shaping of foreign policy.

The NCP hit back with its own allegations against the SPLM. According to one member of the party who had been closely involved in the negotiations and held a senior position in the GoNU, the CPA represented a compromise between unity and separation. Garang's unity agenda won him conspicuous support from the North and turned him into a national figure with a vision and a philosophy. With his death, the SPLM lost a philosopher with a compelling vision. Critical questions about the functioning of the government and the destiny of the nation that should have been directed to the SPLM were being directed to the NCP alone because of the lack of a philosopher in the SPLM or in the Southern leadership. Salva Kiir was perceived in the North as a man who reacted to situations and left without offering answers to questions, which might well have been an underestimation or misreading of the man.

Northern leaders of the NCP and Southerners in Khartoum who were working closely with the NCP all asserted that Southerners had failed in governing their region effectively. Almost verbatim, they all referred to the more than US$1 billion in oil revenues that had been transferred to the South annually and for which there was nothing to show. Even salaries, they said, were not being paid. Some Southerners, including the president, openly alleged corruption, but some diplomatically attributed it to mismanagement, although they also recognized that corruption was rampant as an aspect of mismanagement. They argued that the SPLM was more prone to see wrongs everywhere but in their own actions.

The Yei decisions reaffirming the vision of a New Sudan and a more effective role at the national level tended to be viewed ambivalently by the NCP, accepted as a progressive step but also suspected as a tactical move to draw attention away from the mounting problems in the South. It was also obvious to the adversaries of Garang's leadership in both the North and the South that his image and legacy, in particular the resurgence of his vision, posed a threat to the NCP, especially as it was initially thought that the struggle for a New Sudan had died with him. One senior NCP member argued that it was not surprising that Garang's leadership and his manner of death would lead to a mystification of his legacy in which only the positive was attributed to him. The NCP member, however, saw this as a consequence of Southerners not having credible alternatives.

Although he said that he did not subscribe to the tendency to label those who supported Garang's vision as "Garang's boys," he argued that there were political leaders from the South who did not agree with this reconstruction of Garang's positive image. He was clearly alluding to those Southerners who were opposed to Garang's leadership and remained hostile to his legacy and all it represented. Unwittingly revealing the characteristic divisiveness of the North, he emphasized that divisions in the South, including tribalism, would remain significant factors in the political dynamics of the region. He also noted that the border areas of Southern Kordofan and Blue Nile felt betrayed by the SPLM. In his view, the ability of the SPLM to maintain the unity of the movement would require more than a vision, however legendary. Commenting rather cynically, he thought it expedient of Salva Kiir to resuscitate and promote the vision of Garang, which he described as winning through inaction, a shortsighted tactic that could not be sustained for long.

Interestingly, he looked at the elections as a determining factor without indicating in what direction he thought they might go. He also referred to the election law without elaborating on its significance to the outcome. On the prospects for the South voting for secession or unity, he noted that the NCP was indifferent on the issue and was resigned to whatever the outcome would be. He cited what President al-Bashir had said in his famous Juba statement to the joint meeting of the cabinet and the Legislative Assembly of the GoSS in November 2006, that while the NCP hoped the South would vote for unity, the party would accept a vote for secession and hoped that the North and the South would remain the best of neighbors. With respect to midterm elections, a senior SPLM official intimated to me that one of the decisions of the Yei leadership meeting was to be flexible on the date for the elections, a position on which the NCP and the SPLM might have a mutual interest in preserving the status quo and avoiding the risk of any election results that might upset the arrangements under which they would continue to dominate, although the position was one that observers believed would set a dangerous precedent.

The incremental erosion of the CPA by the NCP was an early indicator that the full implementation of the agreement was uncertain and would continue to be problematic at best. Moreover, the SPLM continued to mark time and refrained from pressing the NCP too hard on issues lest the SPLM might find itself fully "contained," with no power to defend its prized objective—the right to vote for independence.

# Chapter Five: Government of South Sudan

Nowhere can one see the glass more half-full than with respect to the implementation of the CPA at the level of the Southern government. The formation of the GoSS had gone relatively well, but there was an ongoing challenge to be inclusive of all the diverse ethnic groups and to attract the remnants of the militias that had not yet joined the SPLA. Most urgent, however, was the need to make peace dividends visibly available to the people and to embark on robust programs of reconstruction and development. People-oriented programs needed to be designed in such a way as to promote self-reliance and build local capacity to reverse the impact of many years of dependency on international humanitarian assistance. All efforts needed to be made to encourage the South to become a model of constitutional democracy in which elections would be free and fair, with stringent, transparent anticorruption policies, and broad-based people-to-people reconciliation processes were undertaken, building on traditional values, institutions, and practices.

In a short time, and with limited resources, the GoSS made great strides in a number of areas: the adoption of the relevant constitutions at the South Sudan national and state levels; the establishment of the pertinent government ministries, departments, and commissions; the absorption or neutralization of a number of armed groups; the reshuffling of administration and cabinet officials to facilitate good governance and abate corruption; the contribution to regional stability by mediating the peace talks between the government of Uganda and the

LRA; the pursuit of a rigorous legislative agenda; and the commencement of numerous projects aimed at making peace dividends visible to the people.

Despite the ostensible progress made, the GoSS continued to face formidable challenges, including but not limited to the security threats posed by the other armed groups and the proliferation of small arms, delays, and obstacles in bringing the peace dividends to the people, difficulties in taking governance to the local level, and the presence of elements striving to divide the South.

An aspect of South Sudan that posed a formidable challenge to its governance was its ethnic diversity and competitiveness at various levels of the segmentary lineage system that is characteristic of the indigenous social and political order. However balanced and inclusive the efforts to form a government of Southern unity, there were bound to be complaints of discrimination against some groups and favoritism for others.

## Establishment of Institutions and Assignment of Posts

President Salva Kiir was commended for having moved with relative speed and under adverse circumstances to set up the GoSS and put in place the main institutions of government, although a number of institutions and commissions were still to be established in accordance with the Interim Constitution of Southern Sudan.

These included the South Sudan Anti-Corruption Commission, the South Sudan Human Rights Commission, the South Sudan Land Commission, the South Sudan Relief and Rehabilitation Commission (SSRRC), and the South Sudan Demobilization, Disarmament, and Reintegration Commission. During a meeting with the president of Nigeria, Olusegun Obasanjo, and Vice President Ali Osman Mohamed Taha, which I attended, Taha explained the need of the South for expert assistance from African countries, and Obasanjo expressed his country's willingness to offer Nigerian experts to assist in meeting the needs of the South.

A question often posed was whether the right people were appointed to the right positions. After so many years of struggle in which priority was accorded to military functions, political appointments risked rewarding individuals for their dedicated service rather than for competence and professional expertise. Compared to many other African countries at independence, South Sudan had an impressive number of highly educated people. The problem, however, was that their areas of specialization might not correspond to the current needs of the country. It is fair to say that South Sudan was heavy on academic credentials at the higher level, weak on technical expertise at the middle level, and deficient in qualified support staff at the base level. This required programs of special training to develop the needed expertise. The Republic of South Africa was already doing a great deal of training of Southerners in a variety of areas, and similar initiatives were envisioned at all levels.

## Northern Interference in Southern Governance

The North continued support for militias operating in the South. A November 2006 story in the *Sudan Tribune* stated that "corruption, insecurity and bad faith on the part of the Khartoum government in sharing oil profits is slowing Southern Sudan's recovery from years of civil war." Around that same time a public statement by a meeting of Sudanese civil society organizations described the CPA-established National Petroleum Commission as "the most important mechanism towards the realization of equitable oil distribution and revenue utilization." While this might be true, the commission's dysfunction had enabled the NCP to exercise undue influence on the distribution of oil revenues and allowed a lack of transparency to go unchecked. A more positive development was that it was later reported that the outstanding disputes surrounding the commission were resolved by the parties, largely through the establishment of an independent technical secretariat that would be staffed equally by the SPLM and the NCP. The question was whether that agreement would translate into a new commitment by the parties to address, among other things, ongoing oil contract disputes, transparency in oil production rates and revenue distribution, and the participation of civil society in decisions related to oil sector development and revenue utilization.

With respect to Southern governance at the local level, the NCP exerted certain influence as well. More than two years into the interim period, only one Southern state constitution—that of Equatoria—had received the certificate of compliance from the GoNU Ministry of Justice required by the CPA and the Interim Constitution of Sudan. Six others had received comments from the ministry, some of which had been incorporated while others had not. Three Southern states—Unity, Lakes, and Bahr el-Jabal—eventually signed their constitutions into law despite their lack of a GoNU ministry's approval. Some might say that those states were operating unconstitutionally and in violation of the CPA. Others might describe their actions as an exercise in self-determination or a bold defiance of an unreasonable interference by the NCP. In either case, the NCP managed to prevent the Southern states from exercising their self-governance through the legitimate framework of a constitution.

The North also tried to undermine GoSS self-governance by supporting militias in order to impress upon the international community that the South could not peacefully rule itself. This was largely a divide and rule strategy that President Salva Kiir had tackled with a degree of success, especially by having attracted major militia groups, such as the factions under Paulino Matip and Abdel Bagi Ayii, into the SPLM and given them leadership positions in the army (with both Matip and Ayii appointed generals and Matip also appointed the deputy commander-in-chief of the SPLA). Interestingly enough, Ayii and Matip, speaking to me, appeared passionately committed to the struggle for the liberation of Abyei. In their different ways, they both traced their attachment to adolescent experiences: Abdel Bagi was an assistant to an Arab shopkeeper in Abyei, while Paulino Matip herded his cattle in Ngok Dinka land. To Matip, when he took his cattle to graze in Ngok Dinka land, he did not feel as though he was in foreign land; he felt at home. He therefore could not accept Abyei being identified with the North. He said that he had repeatedly pledged to lead the war for the liberation of Abyei. Meeting and discussing the situation in the South with both men was a striking indication of the ironies of the developments in the South. Illiterate as both men were, they posed a serious challenge to the SPLM/A. One SPLM/A leader, referring to Abdel Bagi Ayii, noted that he was a formidable foe of the SPLA on behalf of the SAF. Matip was widely acknowledged as a man who rose from being a retainer of a prominent Nuer chief who was highly admired as a wise leader, to become a high-profile commander of a vast militia army. That these two men could function as leaders of a modern army was surprising, and yet they represented a force that could not be dismissed lightly.

Although the integration of the majority of the militia groups had enhanced the unity and security of the South, there were still armed groups that some of the leading Southerners dismissed as crushable and thus not posing a major threat to the CPA, but they were nonetheless causing insecurity with sporadic acts of violence in and around Juba and other areas of the South. Some of them, however, remained connected to the SAF, were still being supported by the SAF, and continued to engage in activities presumably aimed at undermining the GoSS.

## Bringing Peace Dividends to the People

An area in which the government confronted a serious challenge was in bringing peace dividends to the people who had suffered for half a century from an extremely devastating war. People began to complain that after a year and a half, no peace dividends had been delivered. Ironically, the popular perception was that the GoSS had received sizable amounts of oil money. That perception, unattended to, threatened instability for the country.

Water projects and the delivery of health services had been slow. The roads in Juba, the capital town, were in total disrepair. Sanitation was equally poor, if existent. As the special representative of the secretary-general noted in his September 2006 report, "Southern Sudan remains in urgent need for reconstruction and development assistance. The absence of basic facilities like water, sanitation, healthcare and education has now forced the people to question what difference peace has made in their lives and those of their children."

Accomplishments such as the renovation of government offices, the completion of roads to Uganda and Kenya that facilitated import/export trade, the construction of over 800 schools and the drilling of over 537 water wells (with UN support), and even the notable decrease in food prices in the South were not to be understated. Nor should one minimize the fact that when in Juba, Yei, and other locations, there was a sense of change in the air. Nevertheless, widespread visibility of peace dividends was still falling far short of what was required to close the confidence gap.

To address this situation, First Vice President Kiir opened the second session of the Southern Sudan Legislative Assembly, on September 6, 2006, by delivering a GoSS 200-Day Action Plan that laid out a number of "priority policy actions, activities, projects and programmes that each Ministry had agreed to substantially complete before the end of March 2007." The activities envisioned in the plan were designed to "repair the devastation of war, to rehabilitate and then expand the infrastructure, rebuild and develop the economy, and to re-establish and improve the delivery of essential services to the people."

In many places, the plan was admittedly heavy on the renovation of ministry buildings, the hiring and training of staff, the purchasing of cars and communication equipment, and more planning. These activities, while undeniably indispensable steps in a long-term strategy for development, good governance, and delivery of services, would not be visible to the majority of the populace. The plan, however, contained numerous projects that would be seen and felt by Southern Sudanese who simply wanted to send their children to school, obtain clean water, access medical care, and secure training that would enable them to earn a living. Execution of the plan was to be dependent on a number of factors, not the least of which was international cooperation (as many of the projects were designated to be joint); the institution of efficient mechanisms that facilitated concluding contracts while ensuring against corruption; and public participation and support through increased investment in community-based initiatives, transparency, and public education about the status of planned activities.

Although the needs of the South for relief, the return of refugees and internally displaced persons, and the reconstruction and development of the region were immense, it was sometimes argued that with nearly US$1 billion accruing in oil revenues to the GoSS annually, the problem was not so much a shortage of money as it was mismanagement—in which corruption was a serious threat—and a lack of absorptive capacity. The issue of available revenue, however, should not be underestimated. It was reported, for instance, that while the GoSS budgeted $1.7 billion for 2006 (of which $1.3 million was expected to come from oil revenues), revenues had fallen short. The budget was based on estimated monthly disbursements of approximately $100–$110 million from the GoNU. With no working mechanism for verification, the GoNU informed the GoSS that oil production levels were lower than predicted. As a result, the GoNU monthly payments were closer to $70 million. Moreover, full disbursements from the Multi-Donor Trust Fund (MDTF) (which allocated approximately $300 million to Southern development) were not made.

As for the need to build the requisite GoSS absorptive capacity, in the short run, that could be done by making use of expertise from outside and supporting a program of accelerated training. South Africa had been offering training courses for senior and middle-level officials, including lawyers and police officers. Germany had also been training GoSS jurists. And Kenya was providing intensive English-language training to numerous GoSS officials. Apart from taking Southerners for training abroad, as already planned by USAID, trainers were also sent to the South to train the trainers in programs that would be more cost effective. In addition, to ensure that academic expertise adequately addressed the technical needs of the country, there was an urgent need for the educational system in the South to be more targeted toward the skills required for public administration, including technical fields like engineering, agroindustry, and forestry. Crash programs in these fields needed to be developed.

The reason often given for the inability of the GoSS to make effective use of available funds was a lack of absorptive capacity. While that was a significant consideration, another factor was the power that was given to the World Bank to oversee and manage the disbursement of funds by reviewing contracts and giving approval before execution could be effected. Even such urgent projects as the construction of roads and sanitation in Juba, the capital of the South, were subject to significant delays as a result. The obvious question was whether those regulations that were appropriately intended to guard against corruption should not have been revised to make room for more creative ways of responding more quickly to the postwar demands of the South.

## The Challenge of Corruption

Of course, corruption was and continues to be a major concern in South Sudan. The sources of corruption, as with crime, are multiple and might include need, greed, or adventure. In the case of South Sudan, need and the instinct to make up for lost opportunities in the prolonged struggle could be among the sources. Most of the men in government fought in the jungles of the South for twenty-two years, some of them for forty out of the fifty years of independence. And theirs was a liberation movement that has been described as the poorest ever. One institution they all continued to maintain and value amid all hardships was the family. Some of them, now aging, are rightly concerned about the future of their children. It should also be noted that in Africa generally, and in the conditions of poverty and dire needs in South Sudan in particular, a wide circle of relatives in the extended family and even strangers in one's community or tribe look to the privileged few in leadership positions to provide for their needs. "No" is hardly an answer, since it cannot be believed that a person in that position does not have the means. Failure to help only generates bitterness and discord. Those who maintain high moral standards are both admired and considered failures. Of course, this need not induce corruption in most individuals in leadership positions. It may, however, motivate some officials to look for alternative sources of income beyond their salaries, often through business ventures. That in itself borders on corruption, since it takes away from the time or the focus that should go to public service. It must be remembered that not all those holding public positions have the opportunity to benefit from corruption. Indeed, only a few are well placed to take advantage of the opportunity. But those in that position clearly face strong temptations in the face of need, kinship, and communal pressures for support. It is noteworthy that while a few of those suspected or accused of corruption show evidence of unaccounted wealth, most do not, presumably because whatever they obtain gets diffused into a large social web, kinship obligations in particular.

Allegations of corruption in the South were, of course, rampant and, as noted earlier, were spotlighted by the NCP and their Southern allies who were themselves accused of corruption. All of them often cited the figure of more than US$1 billion of oil revenues that was going to the South annually and for which they alleged there was nothing to show. A respected South Sudanese observer, however, explained that if one considered that 50 percent of the budget of the GoSS went to the army, an allocation that was widely appreciated as necessary to strengthen the SPLA to protect the CPA and the interests of the South, then it should not be surprising that not much showed for the rest of the money.

Concerns regarding corruption or mismanagement of funds were also being expressed by Southerners themselves. In fact, in mid-February 2007, the SPLM gave Salva Kiir "one month to account for 60 million dollars that administration officials claimed was missing from the coffers." During the Yei meeting of the SPLM Interim National Council, the SPLM leaders told Kiir "to sort out his administration which had been accused of corruption and bad management."

The GoSS, whether because of allegations of corruption or to guard against the temptations embedded in the situation, was taking a tough stand in fighting corruption. In his statement to the Donors' Meeting in Juba on March 21, 2007, Salva Kiir stated emphatically, "This is an area [in which] you are all familiar with my stand." He recalled his address at the first Sudan Donor Consortium, "where I promised you to fight corruption in public life with all the might of the law and the will of our people." Toward that end, he announced that the GoSS had established the South Sudan Anti-Corruption Commission and was in the process of drafting relevant legislation, including the Public Financial Management Act. He went on to say, "We will now have institutions with powers to protect public property, investigate cases of corruption . . . and combat malpractices in public institutions."

Of specific significance was the fact that the GoSS "formed a technical team to review all major contracts entered into by GoSS so as to improve our systems and address any malpractices in these contracts." President Kiir reiterated that "there will be no sacred cow when it comes to combating this vice." He cited his "recent decisions" to suspend his minister of finance in order to investigate corruption allegations as a "clear signal to all that there will be no exception when it comes to allegations concerning corruption." Salva Kiir ended his statement on this issue by emphasizing that "corruption is a disease whose affliction is not limited to the Government of Southern Sudan," but "is prevalent, regrettably, all over Sudan." He pledged to champion the "noble task [of fighting corruption] at all levels of our society," and hoped to do that "together with [his] colleagues in the Presidency."

That was compounded by the fact that so much oil money began to flow into the country. But, precisely because the situation appeared ripe for corruption, the leadership of the South was keenly aware of that danger and appeared set to counter it. While that position had been publicly stated by the leaders on a number of occasions, the anticorruption campaign needed to be kept visibly alive, and the public had to be informed on the government's anticorruption policy and actions, and how the money was being spent. A gap, however, continued between the anticorruption rhetoric and effective action against corruption.

While the oversight provided by the World Bank provided a useful watchdog, it was too constraining in the implementation of reconstruction and development projects. For this reason, the WB-managed MDTF might have missed the opportunity at the beginning of the peace to provide the "low-hanging fruit" projects that would have high visibility, such as building schools and health clinics. The MDTF later reportedly tried to address this through a proposed program for "rapid impact projects," which would result in significant disbursements to each Southern state capital that would finance community work projects.

President Salva Kiir made a limited reshuffle of the cabinet and administration in 2006 to enhance good governance and check corruption, a measure that was welcomed and believed to be an interlude to more changes toward those ends. The president also issued a decree appointing the members of the South Sudan Anti-Corruption Commission. The decree was technically not tantamount to the establishment of the commission, which required legislation, the drafting of which had been entrusted to the committee members themselves.

Lastly, as transparency was key to the promotion of confidence in the government, the people needed to be informed about the progress and the obstacles in the provision of services and development. For this reason, continued support needed to be given to UNMIS (UN Mission in Sudan) Radio (which started broadcasting in Juba in June), as well as the new station, Miraya ("Mirror") FM. The free distribution of radios, which USAID was supporting, was an important contribution in this area.

The popular criticism coming from Khartoum, including from those Southerners in the GoNU who were quick to find fault with their GoSS colleagues, was that corruption was rampant. As one of them put it, it was hard to believe that about US$100 million went to the South every month and there was nothing to show for it. According to him, Northerners were happy that the products of this income were not showing, since they would like to see the South remain poor and dependent. While members of the GoSS admitted that there was corruption, they argued that it was not as rampant as was generally alleged. What appeared to be more widely recognized was that there was a sense that Southerners, having been in the jungle for over twenty years, wanted to make up for lost time. Although some had the opportunity to benefit from corruption, more people were inclined to look for business opportunities for making quick money through inflated contracts. The point of intersection between corruption and business opportunities was indeed in government contracts, procurements, and the issuance of licenses.

President Salva Kiir took steps to demonstrate his administration's intolerance for corruption. Evidence of this was his decree suspending the GoSS finance undersecretary, the economic planning undersecretary, the budget director, the taxation director, and the taxation director's deputy over a scandal involving the purchase of government vehicles at inflated prices. Equally promising were the fact that the Southern Sudan Legislative Assembly had established two ad hoc committees to investigate the matter and the fact that the case was also being handled by the GoSS's new Anti-Corruption Commission.

Despite these challenges, the GoSS was in place and striving to function effectively. President Salva Kiir had made changes in his government, including appointing as minister for presidential affairs an internationally respected economist, Dr. Luka Biong Deng, who was already widely acknowledged as having a positive influence on the functioning of the GoSS. Reforms in the organization of work introduced by the newly appointed minister for presidential affairs, including the formation of a ministerial oversight committee, were considered positive steps that should significantly check corruption. This later alienated many with vested interests in Juba, necessitating Luka Biong's transfer to Khartoum as minister of cabinet affairs in the GoNU. He later resigned in protest over Khartoum's invasion of Abyei. In November 2006 the GoSS also released its 2006–11 Aid Strategy, aimed at better coordinating development aid "so that it was used effectively and aligned with the priorities of Southern Sudan." This strategy appeared to have the objective of complementing the budget sector plans of each ministry (such as those stated in the GoSS 200-Day Action Plan) while also ensuring that the GoSS took greater responsibility for the planning, approval, oversight, and accountability related to the implementation of projects funded by aid from all international donor partners.

The GoSS made it clear that the expenditure of aid should be demand led rather than supply driven (that was dictated by the GoSS rather than by the donors). This point was made in particular with respect to capacity building and technical assistance. The GoSS acknowledged that "prolonged conflict and displacement" had resulted in the underdevelopment of the institutional and technical capacity of the government, but that, given the cost of international technical expertise to the donor—particularly in comparison to the cost of local government officials—and the need to build "human capital development" in the South, "the choice of technical assistance and advisors to be provided by development partners, must, in every case rest with the Government [of Southern Sudan]." The GoSS also began to encourage more bilateral agreements to expedite project implementation and ensure increased alignment with GoSS priorities.

Peace appeared to have already boosted the Southern economy to some extent. The "custom market" was booming, allegedly with all the goods available on the East African markets and in Khartoum. An authoritative source reported to me that a great deal more money was floating in Juba than was recognized, presumably because it was unexpected and, in any case, was mostly part of an informal economy that was unaccounted for. Restaurants were mushrooming, catering to international clientele and providing a wide range of cuisines. Hotels were springing up everywhere, which, while providing modest accommodations, were surprisingly expensive. Basic two-room concrete units with running water, flushing toilets, and air conditioning, surrounded by grounds spotted with shady mango trees, formed the Nile Bank–owned Nile Comfort Inn, whose price of $180 a night did not seem to deter even the local residents (mostly employees of the GoSS). Was that a sign of a reverberating economy or a symptom of an ailing predatory society? It was probably both, the real challenge being in what direction the GoSS would steer the economy.

Despite the above, there was little evidence to show that overall conditions were much improved, at least from the perspective of the average South Sudanese citizen. In fact, in a two-day governors' conference held in November 2006 in Juba, the absence of significant construction in and around the South was noted. Roads in Juba were still in utter disrepair or perhaps, more accurately, nonexistent. Sanitation remained appalling. No toilets seemed to work and even the one in the VIP lounge at the Juba airport remained permanently out of order and stinking. At the governors' conference, the "low activity" on the ground was attributed in part to the fact that donors had not fulfilled their original pledges of $2.6 billion, committing only $430 million by November 2006. Some of this was also still attributed to the constraints imposed by the World Bank in the management of the Multi-Donor Trust Funds, which, though understandably intended to guard against corruption, were perceived by many as having the effect of impeding the disbursement of funds and the pace of implementation of urgent projects, such as the construction of roads.

## The Threat of Disunity

One of the persistent paradoxes of being bound by conflicts is the way the Southern political landscape provided a fertile soil for divisive intervention from the North. The popular view was that Northern political leaders believed that there was a price for every Southern politician. The motive of divisive Northern intervention in the South in the CPA context was multifaceted. One aspect was to weaken the SPLM as a political movement. In a discussion with President al-Bashir in the early 1990s on the policies of divisiveness, I argued that this was a short-term military tactic that would not serve the long-term objectives of nation building and that the overriding goal should be to unite the North and the South to reduce the configuration and complexity of conflicting parties. President al-Bashir conceded that in principle that was a noble objective. "But," he said with impressive candor, "you do not expect us to help the South unite in order to be militarily stronger in the field against us."

Related to that was the tactic of convincing friendly Southerners to advance the agenda of the NCP in the South. There was also the desire to prove to the world that the South was divided, backward, and incapable of governing itself, and that without the stabilizing control of the North, it would be a scene of genocidal ethnic conflict akin to Rwanda, or it would disintegrate into statelessness, like Somalia. The objective was to render the South dysfunctional and dependent on the North.

The divisiveness of the North, specifically the NCP, also appeared to be succeeding in fragmenting Southerners in the GoNU. The configuration of Southern ministers in the GoNU could be categorized into those who remained staunchly committed to the principles of the SPLM/A and were in visible confrontation with the NCP; those who were pragmatically cooperating with the NCP and precariously resisting being co-opted; those who had, in fact, been co-opted into the NCP agenda; and those who were independent or belonging to other parties and were engaged in opportunistic alliance with the NCP. This left the unity of the South severely challenged and threatened. These factors contributed to the fissions within the SPLM/A that generated the December 15, 2013, explosion.

## Managing Tribal Conflicts

Conflict in Sudan has always been multilayered, with intercommunal or tribal confrontation rampant at the base level and aggravated by the divisive penetration of the state and the manipulation of ethnic politics by politicians. The intervention of the state in favor of some groups against others undermined the mutual interest in peaceful coexistence between ethnic groups and gave ambitious local politicians and warlords an opportunity for adventure, self-aggrandizement, and material benefit, with much suffering for the ordinary populations.

Foremost among the challenges facing the South was attracting into the SPLM/A the so-called other armed groups that had been used by the NCP government and continued to be supported by the Sudan Armed Forces for counterinsurgency purposes and to divide and weaken the South. While the Juba Declaration of January 2006 brought into the SPLA the main faction of the South Sudan Defense Forces (SSDF) under Paulino Matip, and more groups later joined, there were other groups that continued to be in the ambiguous position of neither joining the SPLA nor becoming absorbed into the SAF.

Additionally, intertribal conflicts in Jonglei, Warrap, and Rumbek were notable sources of insecurity and instability, as were other interethnic tensions resulting from massive population movements. The most serious example of interethnic tension resulting from internal displacement was in Equatoria, where the conflict focused on the reaction of the Equatorians to what they saw as the occupation of their land by the Nilotics, specifically the Dinka. In their eyes, this occupation was only further accentuated by the choice of Juba, their central town, as the capital of the government of South Sudan. The Equatorians felt besieged and their land illegally occupied, particularly by the more than 30,000 Dinka Bor internally displaced persons that were forced to relocate with their herds of cattle to Equatoria during the war. While the Equatorians generally appreciated that the SPLM/A had liberated them from domination by the Arabs, they resented what they saw as the replacement of Arab domination with Nilotic domination. As an Equatorian driver put it to me, "Although the SPLM/A have liberated the South, if we feel that they have replaced the Northerners as occupiers and dominators, why would we vote for an independent South?"

The critical issue of land as a source of ethnic tensions was paradoxically the result of the SPLM's successful defense of the land of the South from the predatory ambitions of the North during the peace negotiations. The SPLM insisted on the principle of community ownership of the land. In fact, it could be argued that this principle was endorsed by the Interim Constitution of Southern Sudan, which recognized customary land tenure that was generally communal. This principle turned out to be a license for the indigenous tribes in the Juba area to reclaim control of the land in Juba and the surrounding areas. The tribes argued that they were not only protecting the land for the community as a whole against the GoSS infrastructure, but also for its individual members who had been displaced but were now expected to return to claim land that had been subsequently occupied by the IDPs from outside the area.

Other Southerners, particularly the Nilotics, were indignant about the attitude of the Equatorians. They referred with a sense of pride to the way the SPLA troops from around the South had protected and eventually liberated the Equatorians from Arab occupation and domination, and saw their attitude as an act of ingratitude. Pointing to the advantages the Equatorians enjoyed in employment by the GoSS and other employers in the capital, they threatened to introduce legislation that would relocate the capital of the South to another area. The paradox was that the Equatorians were opposed to moving the capital elsewhere and yet were not accepting responsibility for having their town be the capital. Non-Equatorians were particularly appalled that the GoSS was not being allowed to use the land in the capital area for public purposes, specifically the establishment of critical GoSS infrastructure. One senior official likened the GoSS to a helicopter hovering over the city and unable to land because people have planted explosives on the landing ground. This is a major issue that still calls for a resolution.

## The Role of the Traditional Justice System

The conflict that erupted on December 15–16 has generated a debate as to whether it is an ethnic conflict between the Dinka and the Nuer. Whatever the truth, the fact that the debate has been generated is enough—there is no smoke without fire. The challenge is to find the fire and extinguish it.

To remedy this trend, it is necessary to encourage a return to the traditional ways of managing and resolving conflicts within a framework of peaceful coexistence. These methods still exist, although their effectiveness has been weakened by the reduced power and influence of the traditional leaders and institutions, and the militarization of society by chronic wars. In the North, the practice by which *ajaweed*, usually prominent tribal chiefs and wise men, are called upon to mediate and resolve intertribal conflicts is still widely resorted to. Throughout the South, peace conferences are a common practice in resolving intertribal conflicts. In recent years, beginning with the Wunlit peace talks between the Dinka and the Nuer, this process has attracted international attention and support. Such support must, however, be carefully managed to avoid dependency on outside resources in what should be affordable, sustainable, broad-based local initiatives in peacemaking.

As with traditional leaders and institutions, the traditional justice system, through customary law, has been weakened by state practice, especially in the conflict of identities that has pitted the Arab Islamic values and institutional practices against indigenous African cultures. While customary law still prevails in most tribal communities, it was viewed by the dominant Northern authorities as primitive, outmoded, repugnant to progress, and above all antithetic to their Islamic vision for the country. By the same token, the war of identities between the North and the South has revived interest in customary law in the South, not only in the administration of justice, but also as a resource for constitutionalism, legislation, and governance. There is still, however, a considerable gap between the aspiration and the practical ways of realizing it.

Projects for recording, restating, reforming, and perhaps codifying customary laws of the various groups in the South were initiated during the interim period and still need encouragement and support. These were initially being conducted and coordinated by the Customary Law Steering Committee under the South Sudan Ministry of Legal Affairs and Constitutional Development. A number of international agencies, including the U.S. Institute of Peace, supported by USAID, were involved in this endeavor. Equally important was the training of judges and attorneys in customary law.

Beyond customary law, there was an urgent need from the beginning to help the South develop a well-functioning administration of justice and respect for the rule of law. War had devastated the infrastructure of the legal system, including courts, prisons, and other institutions. There also was and still is an urgent need for a strong, well-trained, and well-equipped police force to deal with the postwar rise in crime and intercommunal violence.

Recent studies have also revealed appalling prison conditions, arbitrary arrests and detentions, and gross violations of the rights of prisoners and detainees that urgently need to be addressed. In this area, too, Sudan and South Sudan are increasingly seen as mirror images.

## Taking Power to the Local Level

The stability and prosperity of South Sudan also rests on its ability to bring the government closer to the people. This could be done by increasing public exposure and access to the everyday work of the government, as well as through the full establishment and support of local government. Technical and financial support should also be made available to the GoSS Local Government Board. The passage of the Local Governance Act was a priority, as were popular education and support for local government, including capacity-building initiatives and infrastructure development. The UN's commitment to secure communication infrastructure for all Southern state offices by the end of 2006 was a laudable contribution to local governance, as communication problems clearly inhibit and encumber effective government functioning. The car was often the only means of effective communication among government offices and personnel when cell phones failed, which was often the case, and where email access was nonexistent or minimal.

Additionally, local governance could only be effective if the necessary resources were made available to carry out the requisite duties and responsibilities of government. While revenue distribution had begun to trickle down to the local level, it was still far from adequate. For instance, it was reported that Unity State finally got a portion of its 2 percent oil allocation in 2006, which made an incredible difference. The GoSS also transferred $10 million in unconditional grants to each state to pay the civil servants. A ceiling, however, was given as to how many civil employees could be hired. In some states, civil servant numbers exceeded the required limits. Small conditional grants earmarked for certain initiatives were sent to the states, but the amount was so small that little, if any, was transferred to the county level. Technical training and support were needed to facilitate the institution of more efficient and effective mechanisms to deliver payments (particularly in the absence of local bank facilities), control and systematize hiring and pay scales, and provide for greater accounting and transparency in local disbursements of payments.

All in all, considering the formidable challenge of transforming the SPLM/A into a functioning peacetime government after decades of devastating war, the GoSS initially appeared to be performing well. There could, however, be no room for complacency. South Sudan desperately needed the support of the international community to succeed. While the South was still part of Sudan, such a success would provide a check on the excesses of the radical Arab Islamist government at the center. But even separated, the South could still be a moderating influence on Sudan and its Arab Islamic radicalism in the region, especially through alliance with the marginalized regions of Sudan.

The GoSS also suffered from contradictions, ambivalences, and ambiguities similar to those experienced by the GoNU. There were other political parties in the South besides the SPLM, among them the Union of Sudan African Parties (USAP), Sudan African National Union (SANU), South Sudan Democratic Forum (SSDF), United Democratic Front (UDF), United Democratic Salvation Front (UDSF), and SPLM-Democratic Change (SPLM-DC). But, except for the militias that had not joined the

SPLA and some small parties whose leadership remained antagonistic to the movement as a continuation of a personal animosity toward Garang and his legacy, there was a remarkable unity of purpose in the South and a strong support for the SPLM as the champion of the liberation struggle and the achievements of the region under the CPA. Most observers agreed that there was no doubt about the intention of the SPLM to establish a government dedicated to the interests of the people of the South.

Many problems remained unresolved, among them the inadequacy of the governance and reconstruction capacity, the lack of peace dividends, the tendency toward corruption, ethnic factionalism, and the insecurity caused by uncontrolled militias. In many of those areas, the aggravating hand of Khartoum, real or perceived, was a pervasive and persistent factor.

# Chapter Six: The Internally Displaced and Refugees

Within the framework of a united Sudan, and since the partition of the country, internally displaced persons and refugees have been a significant element of the two parts of the country—now the two Sudans—being bound together by conflict. While Sudan did not show much concern for South Sudanese IDPs in the North or for South Sudanese returnees to the South during the war, they showed more interest in South Sudanese in the North after the CPA, even asserting that they were to be treated as Sudanese and not as refugees. Cynics may interpret this as another form of denying their South Sudanese status, or part of the long-standing goal of assimilation into the Arab Islamic identity, and therefore a form of conflict in disguise.

Reports at the time of the study indicated that the parties involved in the programs of IDP returns to South Sudan—the GoNU, the GoSS, the state and county governments, UN agencies, and other humanitarian agencies—had made some inroads in identifying common objectives and strategies for providing to returnees the support services and the security they needed, both en route to and upon arrival at their destinations. However, inadequacies in coordination among the organizations and the organs of government, the politicization of returns, and issues of capacity, resources, and security continued to present obstacles to their efforts. Also complicating the situation were factors relating to the country's terrain and the impediments to transportation caused by the rainy season, especially given the lack of adequate infrastructure. While nothing could be done about the weather, the other obstacles could be overcome with sufficient political will from all sides and the support of the international community. According to the UN Guiding Principles on Internal Displacement, endorsed by the USAID policy on assisting IDPs, return had to be voluntary and conducted in safety and with dignity. The returnees had the right to choose the destination of their return, and all programs of support for reintegration and recovery had to be community based to promote harmonious and cooperative relations between the returnees and the recipient communities.

## The Situation of Return

As was reflected in the reports from Southern Kordofan and Blue Nile, there was notable discrimination in the support that the government of Sudan gave the returnees, favoring Arabs over non-Arabs, who mostly depended on foreign sources of support. At the time the study was conducted, the UN and humanitarian agencies estimated that in 2006 there were over 680,000 returnees going back to the South. Only about 200,000 of those were organized returns, where services and security were provided en route and conditions for sustainable return largely existed upon arrival. The rest were spontaneous returns. There was considerable concern with respect to the 480,000 spontaneous returns and the ability of the GoSS and the respective state governments, communities, and agencies to ensure a secure and dignified passage, as well as to provide the urgent services the returnees would need upon arrival. The fear was that those returns would fail if people found very little waiting for them upon arrival and competition ensued for the scarce resources already needed by the receiving community. Some even elected to go back to the areas of their displacement in the North, only to attempt another return later when even less support was available. In one instance, a community in Khartoum asked the UN to assist it in returning to Upper Nile. The UN informed the group that they would not do that, as conditions there were harsh and not suitable for sustaining returnees. The group disregarded the counsel and returned, only to urgently call upon the UN shortly thereafter and request assistance in moving back to Khartoum because their new environment was devastating.

An interagency effort coordinated by the United Nations Children's Fund (UNICEF) began to provide critical information to IDPs and refugees about the conditions they could expect en route and upon arrival. As print media and Internet were not the most available sources of information, the UN decided to pursue radio access. Unfortunately, the GoNU had not provided UNMIS radio with the license to operate in the North. While UNMIS radio in Juba had been facilitated by the GoSS, UNMIS would not broadcast in the South unless it could simultaneously broadcast in the North.

## Capacity and Coordination

Initially, the visions and work plans of the SPLM and the GoSS differed somewhat from those of the UN and other humanitarian agencies engaged in returns. The GoSS was reported to have set aside about US$24 million to transport approximately 480,000 IDPs back to the South, and was eager to proceed with those mass returns. The international agencies argued that effective return was about more than transportation and that mass returns without adequate preparation and support services could be disastrous, not only for the returnees, but also for the receiving communities and the pertinent authorities in the GoSS and the states concerned. The parties had eventually agreed that returnees required not only transportation, but also assistance and protection en route and upon arrival. Also critical were effective reintegration and recovery programs in the receiving communities.

At the time the study was conducted, it was reported that the SPLM and the NCP were working together to begin the return of displaced Southerners from the North (an estimated 1.8 million to 2 million). The initiative came as a result of a request to the SPLM minister of cabinet affairs in the GoNU, Deng Alor, made by several Southern tribal chiefs residing in the North and wishing assistance for their people to return. The minister approached Vice President Ali Osman Mohamed Taha on the issue and the two agreed to work with the governors of ten Northern states that hosted IDP populations that were seeking return. It was agreed that a special GoNU committee would be formed to organize the return, which the vice president would chair. The success of returns would also depend on the timing, either at the beginning of the rainy season, when planting was opportune, or after the rainy season, when land transport would be easier. Coordination with the UN and humanitarian agencies would also increase the chances that the returnees would move in safety and with dignity and would find a peaceful and potentially sustainable environment upon arrival.

Even here, the cooperation of the GoNU could be said to have been motivated by ambivalence. On the one hand, a significant faction in the North saw the IDPs as a cultural anomaly in the Arab Islamic context and welcomed their return to the South. On the other hand, the presence of Southern IDPs in the North was seen as evidence of their preference for the North over the regime in the South. The area where the ambivalence of the GoNU was most pronounced had to do with ensuring the safety of IDPs and refugees against the Northern communities through which they passed.

## Security Concerns

Security measures were needed to ensure that armed elements did not threaten IDPs or refugee convoys. It might also involve sufficient preparatory work to ensure that returnees would not come into conflict with the communities through which they passed or that would receive them.

Particular concern was raised over the GoNU restrictions on the freedom of movement of UNMIS monitors in areas north of Abyei Town that were well within the Ngok Dinka territory. This restriction, presumably motivated by a fear that such a presence would prejudice the border issues connected with the controversial ABC report, violated the status of forces agreement and created an insecure corridor along a route that was heavily used by spontaneous returnees, not only to Abyei, but also to areas farther South.

Security concerns determined the level of prioritization that IDPs needed to be returned. Where IDPs were at risk or where their presence might lead to an escalation of conflict, their return should take precedence. Conflicts could also be reduced between returnees and the receiving communities by ensuring that social services were equally distributed to members of the receiving community and the returnees. If returnees received benefits and services that the existing communities did not, that could lead to resentment, tensions, and conflict. Information campaigns aimed at educating both returnees and receiving communities about what to expect were critical.

A source of insecurity that was highlighted by Refugees International (RI) as one to which returnees were particularly vulnerable was "landmines and other lethal remnants of the twenty-one-year conflict," which "continue to kill and maim people, obstruct the delivery of humanitarian aid and hinder reconstruction and peace building." According to RI, there might be 500,000 to 2 million mines in South Sudan. Mine clearance therefore had to be a high priority on the postconflict agenda of both the GoNU and the GoSS, with help from the international community.

## Push and Pull Factors in Return

The irony of internal displacement in Sudan was that most Southerners fled to areas controlled by the very government against which their movement was fighting. Generally, Southerners in the North lived normal lives with only subtle, often discreet discrimination. The experience of Southerners who were recognized as IDPs contrasted sharply. For the most part, they were confined to IDP camps or settled in areas where they were treated as subordinate citizens, discriminated against, and often subjected to the arbitrary exercise of law enforcement. Although safety from the war continued to be a major pull factor toward the North, these conditions often acted as push factors for premature returns. With the conclusion of the CPA, pull factors made IDPs in the North want to return. In addition, pressure was exerted from all sides to ensure that returns took place prior to the end of 2007, when the CPA required the completion of the population census that would be critical to the results of the 2009 elections and the 2011 referenda in the South and Abyei. This exerted both push and pull factors on the communities, motivating the GoSS to facilitate their speedy return but making the NCP uncooperative.

South Sudanese in the Diaspora were also confronted with the same pressures and choices as the IDPs in the North. Just how many of them would return in the end was an open question. The Diaspora, however, had an important potential role to play as a source of needed expertise and technical skills.

## Paradoxical Situation of IDPs in Khartoum

Toward the end of 2006, there were approximately 2 million IDPs living in different areas around Khartoum, including four official IDP camps, three planned areas, and three major squatter pockets. In my capacity as representative of the UN secretary-general on internally displaced persons, in my discussions with IDPs at the Mandela Mayo IDP camp on the outskirts of Khartoum that included their leaders, in addition to briefings by several UN staff persons working with these IDP communities on the issues of return, protection, and the provision of services, the surprising message was that life for them in Khartoum had significantly worsened since the CPA. Expectations on the part of the IDPs were raised by the peace agreement that higher levels of assistance would be forthcoming. They also expected support for their return to the South or assistance for relocation in the North. To the contrary, with peace, the level of services previously provided by the government, international organizations, and NGOs had decreased markedly. Violent raids and the forced relocation of IDPs had been carried out by the national authorities. Rampant and indiscriminate harassment for the production of alcohol continued, with imprisonment, sexual violence, and the extortion of large fines as the results.

The IDPs around Khartoum nursed a strong feeling of abandonment, particularly by the SPLM, which had failed, along with the NCP, even to visit the communities and educate them about the CPA and their rights under the agreement and in international law, as well as plans for their protection, reintegration into society (whether that be in the North or in the South), and transfer to the South (if desired). With one resounding voice in my meeting with them, IDPs asked for assistance with transportation, the restoration of assistance from international organizations and NGOs, education for their children, water for their homes, and more specifically, information about the CPA and plans for their return to the South.

Insecurity was a way of life for IDPs around Khartoum. During the period of the study, the police carried out raids on selected camps, relocation sites, and squatter areas around Khartoum. Those raids were regularly accompanied by violence, abuse, and extortions. On August 16 and 17, 2006, authorities violently and forcibly evicted some 12,000 IDPs from Dar es Salaam, south of Khartoum, destroyed about 3,500 houses in a day, and reportedly killed and injured an undetermined number of IDPs during the operations. Despite repeated requests, UNMIS was denied access to the area.

Before the CPA, it was reported that essential services were being delivered to IDP camps. Children received at least one meal a day, there was a greater presence of functioning water pumps, and education (albeit minimal) was available. After the CPA, the government took steps to create conditions that would prompt premature IDP departures by denying them critical services, such as access to clean drinking water, employment opportunities, health care, and education.

Moreover, NGOs previously working in the area either left or decreased their services for a number of reasons, including 1) the reduction of their funds as resources were redirected to the crisis in Darfur, 2) the absence of a comprehensive plan by the parties to facilitate organized returns (which the NGOs could support), and 3) the harassment of aid workers by the authorities.

Interestingly, although the commissioner of the South Sudan Relief and Rehabilitation Commission argued that the North was trying to keep the IDPs as "human shields" to disrupt the census, which he claimed required their return home by June 2007 (as the census had to be completed by July 2007 per the CPA), the NCP authorities appeared to be doing very little to make life appealing in Khartoum.

## Repatriation, Resettlement, and Rehabilitation

As already noted, there was ongoing criticism of the levels of commitment, focus, and cooperation the CPA parties demonstrated on the issues of repatriation, resettlement, and rehabilitation. In the 2002 Machakos Protocol, the parties agreed that there was a need to "formulate a repatriation, resettlement, rehabilitation, reconstruction and development plan to address the needs of those areas affected by the war." Nevertheless, while the July 2004 Joint GoNU Humanitarian Affairs Commission (HAC)/South Sudan Relief and Rehabilitation Commission Policy Framework for the return of displaced persons in a postconflict Sudan was an important step in recognizing the commitment of the parties, it was not sufficient. For this reason, a welcome development was the agreement reached on October 4, 2006, between the HAC and the SSRRC that "foresaw the organized return of up to 150,000 IDPs from Khartoum and the North in 2007, and an additional 50,000 South-South returns and within Blue Nile State."

As a result of the initiative taken by Cabinet Minister Deng Alor in October 2006, strongly supported by Vice President Ali Osman Mohamed Taha and also by President al-Bashir, the government in Khartoum decided to facilitate the return of the displaced populations to their home areas in the South. Regardless of the motivation, the NCP's new position on the situation of IDPs was positive. In his statement to the GoSS leadership during his November 2006 visit to South Sudan, President al-Bashir made a passionate pledge to help the IDPs return to their home areas. Comparing them to refugees who received support from the United Nations High Commission for Refugees (UNHCR), he highlighted the plight of IDPs, and their need for support. The president was seemingly oblivious to the normative principles that placed responsibility for the protection and assistance of internally displaced persons on their governments. According to principle 28(1) of the UN Guiding Principles on Internal Displacement, "Competent authorities have the primary duty and responsibility to establish conditions, as well as provide the means, which allow internally displaced persons to return voluntarily, in safety and with dignity, to their homes or places of habitual residence, or to resettle voluntarily in another part of the country. Such authorities shall endeavor to facilitate the reintegration of returned or resettled internally displaced persons."

With the GoSS intent on helping its people return to the South, and the GoNU now more supportive of that objective, the international community responded positively. In a series of meetings that began in early October 2006 involving the Humanitarian Affairs Commission, the South Sudan Relief and Rehabilitation Commission, the United Nations High Commission for Refugees, the UN Office for the Coordination of Humanitarian Affairs (OCHA), and the International Organization for Migration (IOM), a new cooperation was established to address returns. That new joint plan was characterized by a renewed commitment of resources by all parties.

The displaced populations, IDPs, and refugees, both in their displacement and in the processes of return, resettlement, or integration in the areas of their displacement, represent an ambiguous and ambivalent line between two regions of the country, now the two Sudans. That situation still prevails, now compounded by the flow of refugees in both directions, generated by the conflicts now raging in both countries.

# Chapter Seven: Allegations of Genocide and Mass Atrocities

Sudan has long been accused, wrongly or rightly, of committing genocide and mass atrocities, for which the president, Omar al-Bashir, has been indicted by the International Criminal Court (ICC). Since the December 15–16, 2013, outbreak of violence, South Sudan is alleged to have committed similar crimes, and the UN Security Council has adopted resolution 2206 (2015) on a sanctions regime against South Sudan. Such measures, however, only generate a zero-sum vicious cycle of accusations and denial. There is need for a more constructive approach to the prevention of such atrocities by constructive engagement and management of diversity.

## Demystifying Genocide and Mass Atrocities

The term genocide is often used loosely to describe mass atrocities that may not meet the legal criteria of the 1948 Convention on the Prevention and Punishment of the Crime of Genocide. However defined, genocide is one of the most heinous crimes that humanity should be expected to unite in preventing, halting, and punishing. By the same token, it is a highly emotional issue that is often seen as too sensitive for comfortable discussion, too difficult to touch. Therefore, both the perpetrators and those called upon to prevent or stop it usually fall into denial. That is why we mostly recognize genocide after the fact, in historical hindsight. Prevention before the situation escalates to the point where denial sets in is therefore the best course of action.

It is also critically important to demystify genocide, to shift it from being seen as untouchable, too difficult to deal with, to being more manageably conceptualized as an extreme form of identity-related conflict, whether the groups involved are identified by the factors specified in the 1948 convention, which include national origin, race, ethnicity, and religion, or by some other criteria, including political affiliation.

It must be emphasized that it is not the mere fact of being different that causes genocidal conflicts; it is the implication in terms of how differences are managed, especially the extent to which people are differentiated and politically, economically, and socially stratified. In acutely divided nations, some groups are marginalized, discriminated against, excluded, dehumanized, and denied the dignity and the rights that should normally accrue from citizenship. It is the reaction of these extremely disadvantaged groups that generates a conflict through their resistance to the indignity, a conflict emanating from despair as a result of not having constructive, peaceful alternatives for pursuing equitable belonging to the nation. Resistance then generates a counterreaction that can result in genocide or mass atrocities, depending on the balance of power.

It is paradoxical that the more powerful feel an existential threat from the weaker antagonists, which then motivates them to react with a genocidal onslaught. Unless the perpetrators are defeated militarily, it usually takes the involvement of a third party to mediate, to ensure both equity and face saving. Of course, as noted earlier, the irony of all this is that the subjectivity with which people define themselves, as opposed to the objective realities of their identities, often means that what divides the parties in conflict has a lot to do with myth rather than reality. The people at war are often not as different from one another as they think they are. In a mid- to long-term public policy strategy, this distorted perception needs to be exposed and corrected.

I have been to the former Yugoslavia at the peak of the conflict, to Central Asia amid civil wars, and to a number of African countries undergoing internal conflicts; usually, when you look at the people in conflict, it is not easy to tell who belongs to which side of the divide. I remember addressing crowds in Burundi, some of whom looked typically Tutsi, in a way we are told Tutsis look, and some of whom looked Hutu, but with many, I could not tell whether they were Tutsis or Hutus. I asked the foreign minister after those meetings, "Can you always tell a Tutsi from a Hutu?" His response was, "Yes, but with a margin of error of 35 percent." And that margin of error is common in many parts of the world torn apart by internal conflicts. A Sudanese scholar who heard me tell of this experience commented that in Sudan, especially in regions like Darfur, Southern Kordofan, and Blue Nile, the margin of error would be even larger.

If we take the challenge posed by identity conflicts as one of how to manage diversity constructively, to promote inclusivity, equality, a sense of belonging on equal footing, and pride in being a citizen who enjoys the dignity and rights associated with citizenship, this is an objective that no self-respecting government can question, far less oppose. This is a challenge that provided a positive basis for engagement with governments in my UN mandates on IDPs and genocide prevention.

Diversity is a global phenomenon. Hardly any country can claim to be fully homogeneous. Even Somalia, recognized as one of the most homogeneous countries in the world, has been torn apart by clan differences and conflicting views on Islam. But despite the pervasiveness of diversity, not all countries characterized by diversity experience genocidal identity conflicts. Some manage well, others not so well, and yet others perform dismally. Sadly, Sudan is one of the countries that failed dismally in managing diversity constructively.

South Sudan has struggled for so long in pursuit of ideals of freedom and human dignity, which should now provide a basis for building a system that constructively manages diversity, adheres to the principles of democracy and good governance, respects fundamental rights and civil liberties, pursues equitable socioeconomic development, and promotes gender equality—essential elements of the vision of the New Sudan that the SPLM/A has been championing since its inception. The leaders of South Sudan have struck the right note in all their statements. The challenge is to live up to the commitments made in those statements.

The various conflicts in greater Sudan, Darfur, Blue Nile, Southern Kordofan, and Abyei, and now the internal South Sudan war, have become a major preoccupation for the United Nations. The civil war in South Sudan in particular is eroding the aspirations and robust international support the country enjoyed at independence from Sudan in 2011. This is the case in its relations with the United Nations, and it is also affecting the attitudes of other close friends, allies, and partners in the international community. This need not be the case, especially if we bear in mind the amount of goodwill and solidarity demonstrated by the international community in general, and the United Nations in particular, that contributed to the birth of the young nation.

## The Tortuous Path to South Sudan Independence

Given the strong opposition of Africa and the international community to secessionist movements, the independence of South Sudan was seen by many as a virtual miracle. The event itself was celebrated in Juba with momentous jubilation, and the celebration was attended by many world leaders, including the then president of the UN General Assembly and the UN secretary-general jointly, which was unprecedented. South Sudan was instantly recognized by most countries, with Sudan in the lead. And the speed with which it was admitted to the United Nations, with great enthusiasm, and the jubilation at the hoisting of its flag as the 193rd member state were equally unprecedented.

However, the process leading to the self-determination referendum and independence was not easy. In Africa and throughout the international community, there was considerable skepticism about the viability of an independent South Sudan. Having been intermittently at war for half a century and having never received any significant socioeconomic development, both during colonial rule and since the independence of Sudan in 1956, the country was in dire poverty, landlocked and underdeveloped despite its abundant wealth of natural resources. Its ethnic pluralism, comprising over sixty groups, made many predict that the new country would soon be torn apart by ethnic violence that could spill over into other countries and endanger the peace, security, and stability of the region. Others feared that the independence of South Sudan would be a bad example for Africa, as it would run counter to the commitment of the continent to preserve the colonial borders. I heard these arguments at the AU and in New York at the highest levels and tried to counter them to the best of my ability. Quoting Abel Alier's book, *South Sudan: Too Many Agreements Dishonored*, I argued that if the CPA was dishonored, no peace agreement between the North and the South would be possible again.

Nevertheless, the international community eventually resolved to support holding the referendum on time as stipulated in the CPA and to respect the choice of the people of South Sudan. At a high-level panel convened by the UN secretary-general Ban Ki-moon in September 2010, attended by many heads of state and government, the position of the international community shifted radically in favor of South Sudan's anticipated choice of independence.

After independence was gained on July 9, 2011 international goodwill toward South Sudan continued to grow. Having been in the United Nations Secretariat as special adviser of the secretary-general on the prevention of genocide at the level of undersecretary-general, I witnessed firsthand the strong commitment of the organization, and especially the secretary-general himself, to a robust program of assistance to South Sudan in virtually all critical areas of state building, including security, protection of civilians, provision of essential services, infrastructure, socioeconomic development, and capacity building. The United Nations Mission in South Sudan was the culmination of these ambitious plans, and Hilde Johnson, the former Norwegian minister for international development cooperation who had played an important role in the process that led to the Comprehensive Peace Agreement, was appointed special representative of the secretary-general for South Sudan.

With independence, a myriad of problems, both internal and in Sudan–South Sudan relations, began to emerge that became of increasing concern to the United Nations and the international community at large. The propensity toward violence, a legacy of the long armed struggle, led to many security problems, sometimes against UNMISS staff and other international personnel. The UN began to allege status of forces agreement violations. National authorities also complained about UN staff abuses of SOFA privileges, which they alleged sometimes posed threats to national sovereignty. As the first permanent representative of South Sudan to the United Nations, I heard complaints on both sides and watched the tempers rise. Seen from the perspectives of the parties, the concerns on both sides could be considered valid, but I believe that they were largely due to misunderstandings and that at least some of them could have been more cooperatively addressed through improved communication and constructive engagement.

For instance, the United Nations cannot, of course, be expected to support a rebel movement intent on overthrowing a democratically elected president. But mistakes of the kind that the UN has itself admitted, such as the shipment of arms in UN trucks headed for a warzone that were intercepted, must understandably raise questions and suspicions on the part of the South Sudanese public. Also, while it is inconceivable that UNMISS would have given its vehicles to the rebels, the fact that the rebels acquired possession of ten UNMISS cars with no known resistance or any announcement by UNMISS that their vehicles had been commandeered by the rebels until sometime after the South Sudan government had voiced strong protest also raises serious questions for the government and the public.

Public demonstrations carrying banners and placards, with anti-UN and anti-UNMISS slogans were, of course, expressions of democratic freedom or patriotic responses to these grievances, but they also made South Sudan appear ungrateful for the amount of support the UN had invested in solidarity with the country and its people before and after independence. The leadership of South Sudan fully realized that despite the government's justified grievances, the country had nothing to gain, and much to lose, in antagonizing the UN and, by association, the international community. By the same token, the UN and the international community should appreciate that despite their understandable concerns about the negative developments in the country, South Sudan, as a new nation, faces many daunting challenges and desperately needs their support, whatever the differences between them created by the current crisis.

As South Sudan was already rendered vulnerable by half a century of war, the violence that erupted on December 15 and 16, 2013, and that escalated into an internecine civil war pitting kindred groups against one another, has made the country even more vulnerable than it ever was. South Sudan needs the sympathy, the solidarity, and the support of the international community even more now than it ever did before. The role of the United Nations is pivotal in this global partnership.

Even in this crisis, there is much for which the government and people of South Sudan should be grateful to the UN. It is not difficult to imagine what South Sudan would have been without UNMISS in the current crisis. By opening its compounds to protect those fleeing from imminent death—the first time the UN has done so—UNMISS has saved the lives of probably thousands of South Sudanese. In addition to protecting civilians, the UN and its partners are actively engaged in providing badly needed humanitarian assistance. They are also supporting the IGAD-AU peace process. There are, however, genuine concerns on both sides that need to be candidly and constructively discussed and addressed.

Whatever the justification for the popular anti-UN demonstrations, the leadership of South Sudan and the United Nations should continue to strive to promote mutual understanding and cooperation between the government of South Sudan and the UN, through better communication and constructive engagement. As the permanent representative of South Sudan to the UN, I firmly believe that bridging conflicting positions is the challenge of diplomacy, by whichever means it is pursued, preferably through dialogue.

## The Challenge to South Sudan's Diplomacy

In view of the crisis that South Sudan is going through, its implications for the foreign policy of our country, and what South Sudanese diplomats are expected to do in projecting the official position of the government to the outside world, I thought that I should include in this volume a concept note I prepared when my country honored me to be its first permanent representative to the United Nations. In that note,

I outlined my understanding of the principles that underlie diplomacy and how I planned to pursue my assignment. What follows is a revised version of the concept note I prepared then and shared with the presidency and the Ministry of Foreign Affairs and International Cooperation.

The premise of my approach was that diplomacy is a strategic means of pursuing the objectives of the nation's foreign policy. South Sudan's foreign policy is laid out in the Transitional Constitution of South Sudan. The relevant provisions of the constitution state the following:

> Foreign policy of the Republic of South Sudan shall serve the national interest and shall be conducted independently and transparently with the view to achieving the following:
>
> a) promotion of international cooperation, especially within the United Nations family, African Union, and other international and regional organizations, for the purposes of consolidating universal peace and security, respect for international law, treaty obligations and fostering a just world economic order;
>
> b) achievement of African economic integration, within the ongoing regional plans and as well as promoting African unity and cooperation as foreseen in those plans;
>
> c) enhancement of respect for human rights and fundamental freedoms in regional and international fora;
>
> d) promotion of dialogue among civilizations and establishment of international order based on justice and common human destiny;
>
> e) respect for international law and treaty obligations, as well as the seeking of the peaceful settlement of international disputes by negotiation, mediation, conciliation, arbitration, and adjudication;
>
> f) enhancement of economic cooperation among countries of the region;
>
> g) non-interference in the affairs of other States, promotion of good-neighbourliness and mutual cooperation with all neighbours, and maintenance of amicable and balanced relations with other countries; and
>
> h) combating international and trans-national organized crime, piracy, and terrorism.

The purpose of the concept note was therefore not to formulate the foreign policy of South Sudan, but to expound on the strategic approach to the implementation of the stipulated policy.

The first premise of that approach is that foreign policy is an extension of domestic policy and that a diplomat ideally should have a positive domestic "commodity to sell" in promoting international cooperation. As ambassador and minister of state for foreign affairs in the government of Jaafar Mohommad Nimeiri, I was able to build on the achievement of the 1972 Addis Ababa Agreement and the strategic shift from violent conflict to managing diversity constructively and promoting equitable development. The challenge for our foreign policy was to gain support for these domestic achievements and objectives, which made Sudan a positive model regionally and a strategic partner internationally. When Nimeiri abrogated the Addis Ababa Agreement and undid those positive achievements and objectives, I resigned from the government.

My second premise was that diplomacy is primarily an art of negotiating human relations and that governments and organizations are represented by individual human beings whose personal identity, pride, and dignity become closely associated with the institutions they represent. To me personally, as someone who has devoted a great deal of intellectual work to understanding the cultural values of South Sudan's traditional society, I believe it is important to build on South Sudan's indigenous values, even in international relations. The values of persuasion, consensus building, respect for others' points of view, and face saving are central to the objective of peaceful resolution of conflicts in South Sudan's traditional society. To a degree, I believe these are also universal values.

Those two conceptual premises lead to two major operational implications. The first is that South Sudan must have a positive domestic policy framework on which to base its foreign policy strategies. Ensuring international support for the full and credible implementation of the Comprehensive Peace Agreement was one such framework. The second implication is that South Sudan must be projected as a model of good governance that aims to correct the shortcomings of the old Sudan by achieving the objectives of the postulated New Sudan vision. This should entail ensuring democratic participation and constructive management of diversity based on the principles of nondiscrimination, inclusivity, respect for fundamental rights and civil liberties, and promotion of human dignity for all, irrespective of race, ethnicity, religion, culture, and gender.

This should make South Sudan attractive to the diverse peoples of the region and the continent, a process that had already begun because of the opportunities this nascent country was providing. In this connection, South Sudan should guard against xenophobia, which often results from the influx of foreign workers with manpower and expertise to contribute to the development of a country.

The second is that one must engage both potential partners and adversaries through constructive dialogue, mutual respect, and persuasiveness, rather than acrimonious confrontation. In other words, quiet diplomacy might be more constructive than public, confrontational acrimony. This does not, however, mean concealing "confrontational" facts. But where facts represent unavoidable confrontation, they need to be presented in a dispassionate, objective, principled manner that is more likely to win support from third parties than loud acrimonious verbalism. This is not to dismiss the value of the confrontational approach when circumstances warrant, but that approach should be resorted to sparingly and as the context demands. In any case, there are political voices whose role is more suited to the confrontational approach than to diplomatic representation.

These principles obviously operate differently in the contexts of bilateral and multilateral diplomacy. The first context involves two countries and the individuals representing those countries. The second is more complex as it involves regional and international dynamics, in addition to dealing with different departments, agencies, and programs of the United Nations system.

The guiding principles should, however, be the same in both contexts, although the manner in which they are operationalized and implemented will vary. The role of diplomats in the bilateral context will, of course, focus on soliciting cooperation with individual member states and the UN system to assist in the delivery of services and socioeconomic development of South Sudan. The role of diplomats in multilateral diplomacy will be more discreetly reflected in our influence in shaping regional and international perspectives and positions, to a degree based on our national interests and policy orientation. In this process, the role of a diplomat should be one of a bridge builder not only through the credible transmission of messages, but also by offering advice on policy and appropriate strategies.

It should be noted that while official bilateral and multilateral interlocutors are critical to our diplomatic focus, there is a much wider circle of potential influence that needs to be reached and tapped. Among these are academic and research institutions, think tanks, civil society organizations, and influential international partners. Since my own work over the years, in and out of government, brought me into close contact with elements of these circles, I planned to make effective use of them in support of our foreign policy objectives and strategies.

In the foreseeable future, South Sudan's relations with Sudan will be one of the most challenging issues for South Sudan diplomacy. This will center on the proliferating regional rebellions in Sudan, in particular the SPLM-North, and their relationship with South Sudan. As I see it, we must endeavor to shift international attention from the alleged support of South Sudan for Sudan's rebel movements to addressing the genuine grievances of the groups they represent through a negotiated settlement between them and the government, with South Sudan using its good offices, rooted in the close connection with these groups, to assist Sudan by mediating a peaceful resolution of the conflicts. After all, although the Nuba of Southern Kordofan and the Ingessana of Blue Nile fought alongside the South, they were not fighting for the cause of Southern independence, but for their own cause, albeit in alliance with the South. On the other hand, as allies who contributed significantly to the success of the South Sudanese to achieve their objectives, South Sudan has a moral and indeed a political obligation to assist them in pursuing their legitimate objectives through peaceful means, in cooperation with Sudan and with the support of the international community.

What all this means is that our role as diplomats and specifically at the Mission of South Sudan to the United Nations should be to expound on, and contribute to, positive national policy, goals, objectives, and principles on which to build our diplomatic approaches: map out the circles we need to target and win support of our domestic agenda; use persuasive means of countering adversarial messages and gaining international support for our positions; solicit cooperation from UN departments, specialized agencies, programs, and funds for our socioeconomic development; play an effective role in regional, subregional, and other multilateral circles to influence positions in accordance with our domestic principles and policy framework; and, through a two-way process of mutual influence, benefit from the perspectives of our international interlocutors.

Although we have endeavored to influence the Security Council in its consideration of sanctions against South Sudan, as it has decided on a sanctions regime, the challenge is now one of creating conditions that will persuade the UN to lift the sanctions, suspend their imposition, or defer their implementation. This means that instead of a hostile reaction to the sanctions, as some are prone to, we should develop cooperative efforts toward peace, which is the purpose of the sanctions regime against South Sudan.

## The Crisis in Perspective

The crisis of national identity and the persistent failure to manage diversity constructively since independence confront Sudan and South Sudan with several contextual challenges.

First, the independent South Sudan must correct the mistakes of the past by adopting a South Sudan national identity framework that promotes inclusivity, equality, and dignity for all ethnic groups without discrimination—a New Sudan in the South Sudan context.

Second, neither Sudan nor South Sudan can be indifferent to the genuine grievances of disadvantaged and marginalized groups in their respective contexts, but, as President Salva Kiir said in his Independence Day speech, they should help each other cooperatively to address these grievances to promote peace, security, stability, and equality for all.

Sudan must address the grievances of these regions by adopting the principles embodied by the New Sudan in the Northern context. This should ensure regional autonomy similar to what South Sudan enjoyed during the CPA interim period, without the option of separation, but with equitable participation at the center.

Third, the cause of the people of Abyei that has driven them to join South Sudan in the two wars between the North and the South, and that has been recognized in several agreements, must be effectively addressed by implementing the Abyei Protocol of the CPA and the findings of the Permanent Court of Arbitration (PCA), or it will continue to threaten peaceful and cooperative relations between Sudan and South Sudan.

Fourth, South Sudan, being one of the African countries least affected by modernity and the blanket importation of outside models of governance, must endeavor to make effective use of its indigenous cultural values, institutional structures, and patterns of behavior, as the essence of genuine self-determination. These indigenous principles can be used effectively in developing norms and operational measures for conflict prevention, management, and resolution; reinforcing international human rights standards; promoting equitable socioeconomic development; and reforming gender relations toward mutual respect and equality between the sexes.

Fifth, South Sudan has been the beneficiary of the United Nations and the international community at large and must strive to live up to international standards of good governance, respect for human rights, and humanitarian principles, and be responsive to the concerns of the world body and major actors about violations in these areas. Constructive and productive engagement must be the basic norm.

Sixth, although sanctions hardly ever achieve their intended objectives, but instead tend to hurt innocent civilians, we must avoid the temptation of a hostile response, and must endeavor to intensify efforts toward peace, which is the objective of the sanctions against South Sudan in the first place.

Finally, it is in the interest of both Sudan and South Sudan to resolve their internal conflicts and improve their bilateral relations toward some form of association that would foster regional peace and cooperation. The alternative will be instability and perpetual conflicts within and between the two countries.

The international community should approach the conflicts within and between Sudan and South Sudan regionally along the lines of the Great Lakes Region's peace process to promote internal and regional peace, security, and stability.

# Conclusion

This book has tried to substantiate two complementary themes. The first is that the current crises in South Sudan have their roots in the unfinished job of the CPA implementation between Sudan and South Sudan. The second is that the internal conflicts in the two countries interplay across the borders to fuel ongoing interstate conflicts. Two implications emerge from these themes. First, the full and credible implementation of the CPA is a necessary condition to peaceful and cooperative relations between the two countries. Second, unless the two countries resolve their internal conflicts to achieve and consolidate peace, security, and stability within their borders, their relations will continue to be threatened by the interconnectedness of conflicts across their borders.

The critical question then is how these internal conflicts can be effectively resolved. This depends on how the causes of these conflicts are perceived. I remain convinced that the regional conflicts in Sudan between the center and the periphery emanate from an acute crisis of national identity. The core of this crisis is that the African Arab hybrid that has monopolized power perceives itself as Arab Islamic and imposes this distorted self-perception on the multiracial, multiethnic, multireligious, and multicultural composition of the country and defines it as Arab Islamic, which inevitably discriminates against the non-Arab and non-Muslim fellow Sudanese.

The strategy for resolving this crisis is the constructive management of diversity toward a system of constitutionalism and governance that promotes equality, inclusivity, and nondiscrimination and respect for the humanity of all groups without distinction based on race, ethnicity, religion, culture, or gender, the vision of a New Sudan postulated by the SPLM/A.

Although the challenge for the South also concerns the constructive management of diversity toward inclusivity, equality, and nondiscrimination, the dynamics are different. Unlike the dualism in Sudan between the dominant Arab Islamic group and the marginalized non-Arab and non-Muslim groups, the pluralism of South Sudan is more egalitarian. Not only do all South Sudanese ethnic or tribal groups enjoy self-esteem that does not recognize or allow the dominance of any one group, but, given the potential dynamic alliances among the many ethnic groups, no one group can claim a dominant majority over all the others. Nor are there any of the clear distinguishing racial, ethnic, religious, and cultural identity factors that dichotomize the groups in Sudan.

What then is the solution for the interethnic conflicts in South Sudan? In determining the precise system that will suit South Sudan, it is important to remember the organizational structure of traditional South Sudanese society, which pioneering, world-famous anthropologists have studied and documented in great detail. The technical terms used to describe these societies are "acephalous," "segmentary," "ethnocentric," "stateless," and "ordered anarchy." Put in simple terms, these are very proud, egocentric, and egalitarian people who will not allow anyone to lord it over them, to paraphrase the language of the late Professor Sir Edward Evans-Pritchard, who was the world's leading anthropologist and specialist on the Nuer, the kindred of the Dinka. Sadly, his writings, which no student of anthropology can escape from, have tended to lay emphasis on Dinka-Nuer historic animosities, grossly exaggerated and even subjective, but self-fulfilling and mutually reinforcing.

Although the traditional system of governance recognizes a hierarchy of leadership with great respect and deference due to traditional leaders, the autonomy of groups, down to the level of families and the individual, was the core principle of the indigenous system. Leadership was largely a mediator in managing conflicts and not an imposer of authority. The effectiveness of leadership was due to the wisdom of decision makers, which eventually provided consensus. Consensus was indeed the foundation of constitutional democracy in traditional Dinka and Nuer societies, and, I believe, in most South Sudanese and indigenous African systems.

Of course, traditional principles of governance can no longer be applied effectively in the modern complex system of government. But cultural values run deep, and while society must adjust to the dictates of the modern world, it must also respect the fundamental cultural values and sentiments that are deeply entrenched in the people, even as they change.

A major flaw in the modern constitutions of African states is that they are essentially Western models that were thrust on the newly independent states in Africa, even though the democratic ideals they embodied were not observed, far less applied, by the colonial rulers. These constitutional models were not designed to build the constructive management of diversity. The closest to managing diversity was the accommodation of traditional administration through indirect rule, which utilized tribal leaders or chiefs as a less costly way of administering rural areas. Even this was a means of ensuring security, law, and order at minimum cost to the colonial government.

The details of a devolution of powers along the lines of a segmentary system can be developed and negotiated by a multidisciplinary group of experts. The overriding goals must be for all South Sudanese ethnic groups to feel self-governing, included in the national governance system, and to partake in an equitable distribution of resources. It would be ironic for South Sudanese to allow themselves to be divided by the identity conflicts against which they struggled for over half a century in order to create a New Sudan of full equality, without discrimination on the basis of race, ethnicity, religion, culture, or gender.

Confederalism, federalism, autonomy, self-government, proportional representation, minority rights, and other symmetrical and asymmetrical power arrangements all remain viable models for addressing ethnic conflict, sharing power, and addressing self-determination demands.

They all focus on mechanisms for sharing power and resources equitably within the country and, where necessary, to devolve power from the center to all or a portion of the periphery. Any one of these arrangements can be effective if it allows the people in question to secure an equitable role at the national level, to preserve their identity, to determine their destiny, and to take greater control over decisions affecting their own economic, social, and cultural development.

What is required is not a well-written, ideal constitutional document, but a system of constitutionalism that gives a spirit and life to the document. In the end, it is not the name that is important, but the fact that the people of the nation have sat down together, deliberated with one another, identified their objectives, reached common understandings, and designed a structure that meets their mutual aspirations. The result may mimic existing models and would still be constructive, and if the governing framework results in something that the world has not yet seen, that too would be a constructive contribution. In a speech delivered at the Third International Conference on Federalism in Brussels on March 5, 2005, John Garang de Mabior outlined the main principles of Sudan's CPA and concluded that the agreement was a "unique Sudanese achievement" that defied being labeled as one or another of the conventional constitutional models. "Now that the child has been born," he told his audience, "you can decide what to call the form of governance that we have agreed to in the CPA, whether it is a federation, confederation, true federalism or some other 'ism.'" Although he considered the CPA a unique Sudanese solution to a costly and protracted war, he also believed that its influence would be positive for Africa.

Judging from recent developments, the signs are not encouraging, and there is a clear need for greater creativity in the search for viable solutions. On the other hand, the mere fact that it was possible for the CPA to be concluded and implemented to result in the independence of South Sudan is a remarkable accomplishment in the African context. However, some of the predictions of doom that were intended to discourage South Sudanese independence seem to be proving to be self-fulfilling prophecies. Sudan and South Sudan now face the challenge of changing the mind-set of conflict that still negatively binds them together and working for genuine cooperation in addressing their internal and cross-border conflicts that will continue to threaten their bilateral relations. This is the core of the title of this book—*Bound by Conflict: Dilemmas of the Two Sudans*. If this book adds to the debate on the issues involved within and between the two Sudans, I would consider it a gratifying success.

## APPENDIX: STATEMENTS TO THE UNITED NATIONS

This appendix includes statements I made to the Security Council and other UN entities since assuming the position of permanent representative of South Sudan to the United Nations in September 2012. The statements cover themes that relate to the crosscutting areas that have been of major concern to the United Nations and therefore to our mission and that have been the focus of this book. They include relations between Sudan and South Sudan, the role of the United Nations Mission in South Sudan (UNMISS), the role of the United Nations Interim Security Force for Abyei (UNISFA), and the rebellion/civil war in South Sudan that ensued after the December 15, 2013, outbreak of hostilities in Juba.

As the book argues, these areas interplay and aggravate one another. Sudan–South Sudan relations are affected by the situation in Abyei and the challenging protection role of UNISFA on their borders, pitting the Ngok Dinka against the Missiriya Arabs, who are supported by Sudan's army and militias. UNMISS faces similar protection challenges on the Sudan–South Sudan borders, where SPLM/N forces clash with the Sudan Armed Forces in hot pursuit of the rebels, whom Khartoum believes are being supported by South Sudan. Conversely, it is now reasonably well established that Sudan is supporting Riek Machar's rebels, which is worsening the relations between Khartoum and Juba that had recently improved.

Among the areas of particular concern to the UN system are the challenges of protecting of civilians, especially IDPs in UNMISS camps, international concerns about violations of human rights and humanitarian law, alleged restrictions on humanitarian access, recruitment and use of children as soldiers, sexual violence and other gender-related abuses of women and girls, protection of UN personnel and their equipment and installations, and the overall controversy over the application of the status of force agreement. These have all contributed to tensions between South Sudan and the UN. Added to that is the continuing and intensifying violence in the war between the government and Riek Machar's rebel forces. As the IGAD mediation appears to be stalling, the search for ways of reinvigorating those efforts becomes a preoccupation for the UN and the international community.

All these factors have contributed to the rising level of frustration in the international community, which has prompted pressure for the imposition of sanctions on individuals and entities who are deemed responsible for impeding progress toward peace. Our position has been that sanctions hardly ever accomplish their intended objective; quite the contrary, they tend to harden positions and encourage confrontation. If the targets are leading personalities needed in negotiations, that would undermine the peace process. If, on the other hand, they are middle-rank individuals with no crucial role in the peace process, then sanctions would be an exercise in futility.

Despite recent differences and disagreements, both the South Sudanese government and its people remain deeply appreciative of the support they received from the international community for the cause of their independence and for the postconflict reconstruction and development of South Sudan, and this gratitude gives them high moral authority and leverage to pressure the parties for peace through constructive engagement and not through the threats of sanctions or punitive measures. It is ironic that it was the United States that led the call for sanctions, when it was the country that played a pivotal role in support for the independence of South Sudan and for postwar reconstruction and development of the country. It is therefore the country with the greatest potential leverage to influence the parties through dialogue and constructive engagement. Interestingly enough, the United States also uses the moral and political investment it has made in the South and its commitment to the country and the people as the reason for what one might call its "tough love" approach. But arguably, it can achieve positive results through one more conciliatory approach. Together with the other members of the Troika, the UK and Norway, and with the involvement of China, it can still play that role and leave pending the actual implementation of the sanctions regime.

These are the issues that these statements address, and while there is a considerable degree of recurrence in the themes, I hope that they add a significant dimension to the thesis of the book and that they are not unduly repetitive.

## 1. Statement by Dr. Francis Mading Deng, Permanent Representative of the Republic of South Sudan to the United Nations, during Its Consultations on Sudan and South Sudan, New York, November 28, 2012

Mr. President,

This being my first time to address the Council in my new capacity as Permanent Representative of the Republic of South Sudan to the United Nations, I would like to personally express my appreciation for the opportunity and to congratulate you, Mr. President, for your Presidency this month.

I would like to thank the Under-Secretary-General for Peacekeeping Operations for his briefing that he has just presented, and also thank the Special Representative of the Secretary-General, Hilde Johnson, as well as the Special Envoy, Haile Menkerios, for their hard work in support of peace and security in South Sudan and Sudan. Furthermore, I would like to express my appreciation to His Excellency, Secretary-General Ban Ki-moon, for his comprehensive and balanced report outlining the successes as well as the ongoing challenges in the maintenance of peace and security between Sudan and South Sudan. Establishing a comprehensive and sustainable peace with the Republic of Sudan is our government's number one priority.

The Republic of South Sudan would also like to reiterate its appreciation to the members of the Security Council for their support of the roadmap established by the African Union Peace and Security Council on 24 April 2012, and the importance this Council places on the leading role that the African Union plays in the promotion of peace and security in our region.

Mr. President,

The leaders of Sudan and South Sudan have long agreed, as far back as the signing of the Machakos Protocol in 2002, that war would never represent a viable solution to ending the conflicts between them, and that negotiation remains the only worthwhile approach. At the same time, negotiation without end is in no one's interests. Our two states cannot prosper or pursue greater development in an atmosphere of continued uncertainty about their relations. It is for this reason that the AU Roadmap and Security Council Resolution 2046 helpfully established deadlines for the resolution of all the outstanding issues between our two states. Both the AU Roadmap and Resolution 2046 created an opportunity for our two countries to resolve the outstanding issues definitively. Resolution 2046 also called on the Secretary-General, in consultation with the African Union and IGAD, to issue binding proposals on any issues on which the parties could not agree within the reasonable deadline that was established by this Council.

The Republic of South Sudan appreciates the efforts of the African Union High Level Implementation Panel comprising their Excellencies President Thabo Mbeki, President Pierre Buyoya and President Abdulsalami Abubakar, all of whom tirelessly supported the parties during this Summer's negotiations, and who provided the required continental context and political support to enable the creation of African solutions for the establishment of peace and stability in the region.

Mr. President,

The agreements signed by the parties on 27th September are welcome and represent an important milestone, defining in concrete terms the future relations between our two states. However, as this Council itself recognized when it unanimously passed Resolution 2046, what is required, some seven years after the signing of the Comprehensive Peace Agreement, is final resolution of all of the outstanding issues that remain between us. My government signed the cooperation agreements on 27th September because we were convinced that it would be possible quickly to resolve the matters on which we could not agree on that day, most importantly border demarcation and the status of Abyei. We would welcome this Council's continued and active support of this objective, in full cooperation with and support of the African Union. It is only when all of the issues are addressed, and we have made much greater progress towards the full implementation of key provisions of the 2005 Comprehensive Peace Agreement, that sustainable peace will exist in our region. There are no shortcuts to this destination.

It is with this in mind that we respectfully ask this Council to support unreservedly the AU Peace and Security Council decision of 24th October 2012. As you are all aware, the AUHIP's 21 September 2012 proposal on the final status of Abyei reflects the previous agreements signed by the parties, such as the Abyei Protocol of the 2005 CPA, the arbitration agreement that led to the 2009 award of the Permanent Court of Arbitration tribunal, and the 20th June 2011 agreement. These agreements provided the foundation for the AUHIP's approach to the discussions on Abyei over recent months. All of these agreements accept the need to hold a referendum in the Abyei Area. A referendum, implemented in accordance with the terms of the CPA, does not represent a win/lose solution for that area's communities. To the contrary, to the extent that it would ensure peace, security and restore peaceful cooperation between the communities, it would be a win-win situation.

That said, following the decision of the AU Peace and Security Council on 24th October, my government expressed its readiness to negotiate with Sudan for a further six weeks. H. E. President Salva Kiir Mayardit formally invited H. E. President Omer-Hassan El Bashir to Juba in order to continue their discussions on the final status of Abyei. We regret that President El Bashir has been unable thus far to take up this invitation. The deadline established by the AU PSC is now approaching and it is our hope that the efforts exerted by my government to negotiate on the basis of the AUHIP's last proposal, as well as to establish the temporary institutions of the Abyei area, will be supported both by the members of the PSC and by this Council. The Republic of South Sudan would also welcome the endorsement of the UN Security Council of any decision made by the African Union with regards to Abyei or other outstanding issues, not as an imposition on the parties but rather as a demonstration of support for the region's considered view of what the most appropriate way forward is.

The Republic of South Sudan is also eager to implement the security mechanisms, namely the Safe Demilitarized Border Zone and the Joint Border Verification and Monitoring Mechanism, without further delay. My Government continues to be extremely concerned by the humanitarian impact that the conflict in Southern Kordofan and Blue Nile has on the people of these areas, and indeed by extension on the people of South Sudan, who have so far welcomed over 100,000 refugees from this conflict. As the Secretary-General notes in his recent report, and I quote: "the human suffering in the two states is a direct consequence of the conflict in those areas. Only a resolution of the conflict can stop the humanitarian crisis."

As the Council is aware, in connection with the insecurity in the Two Areas, Sudan has recently conducted aerial bombardments inside the territory of South Sudan, specifically in Northern Bahr El Ghazal State. The Republic of South Sudan does not wish to return to violence, and remains fully committed to peace. We do not believe that there can be genuine security in the border states of either country, and therefore sustainable peace in our region, unless there is a complete cessation of hostilities in the Two Areas. We therefore strongly encourage dialogue between the Government of Sudan and the SPLM-North, as called for in Resolution 2046, and offer ourselves to the parties to play whatever facilitating role might be deemed necessary. It is clear that unless there can be a dialogue on the basis of previous agreements, including the CPA and last year's 28 June agreement, it will be difficult to implement the Safe Demilitarized Border Zone (SDBZ) and Joint Border Verification Monitoring Mechanism (JBVMM).

Mr. President,

The Republic of South Sudan continues its preparations for the resumption of oil production and the transport of oil through the territory of Sudan, despite calls by Sudan to halt these preparations, and its imposition of additional demands on security issues that go far beyond the scope of the 27th September agreements. We are nonetheless encouraged by a recent exchange between our two Presidents and an agreement to reconvene the Joint Political and Security Mechanism in Khartoum next week.

Mr. President,

Whilst relations with Sudan occupy the highest priority on my government's agenda, the situation in Jonglei State remains an acute focus. On Monday, President Salva Kiir reiterated that his Government would spare no effort in support of stability and inter-communal harmony in Jonglei. My Government is pursuing a multi-pronged strategy in Jonglei. The peace process is being led by a Presidential Committee on Peace, Reconciliation, and Tolerance in Jonglei State and the disarmament process is being led by the SPLA. Despite some very concerning reports about the conduct of the SPLA in isolated situations, the civilian disarmament process has largely been conducted peacefully. The Government takes any allegations of misconduct by the SPLA very seriously. All allegations will be investigated and if necessary will be addressed through the appropriate legal mechanisms and channels.

The Government has gone to great lengths to facilitate contact between the different communities in Jonglei State. Both the reconciliation process and the disarmament process have been welcomed by the communities in Jonglei State, as has the SPLA's pledge to remain on the ground in the state for up to two years to provide ongoing security. The Sudan Council of Churches also continues a grassroots peace process to complement the government-led process.

We welcome the support that UNMISS has provided to the Jonglei peace process, and would welcome enhanced logistical support, as well as ongoing support of the implementation of the May 2012 peace agreements signed in Jonglei.

Mr. President,

We note the concerns expressed by several members of this Council and just also articulated by the Under-Secretary General regarding the expulsion of a Human Rights Officer who served with UNMISS. Whilst South Sudan takes these concerns very seriously, it is our belief that we acted consistently with the UNMISS SOFA. The Republic of South Sudan does not intend to hinder human rights reporting in South Sudan and accepts this as an integral component of the work of UNMISS.

We also welcome ongoing negotiations and dialogue on these issues and I might add here that initially 2 were expelled including the director, but as a result of discussions with the leadership, that decision, regarding one, was reversed. I should also say that the relevant institutions within the Ministry of Foreign Affairs and other legal institutions have conducted thorough analysis of relevant international conventions and norms in order to give legal basis to the decision made. We do believe, therefore, that contrary to the allegations, the decisions were not taken lightly nor in disregard to the relevant international conventions.

We indeed want to underscore here our unwavering commitment to international human rights and humanitarian standards. The war that raged in our region intermittently for half a century was a struggle for human rights and the values of human dignity. We recognize that there is always a gap between ideals and practice on the ground and in this area, we endeavour to do more. I indeed noted with great interest some of the specifics cited by the Under-Secretary General of instances which indicate the gap that I am referring to. And once again, we are quite willing and prepared to discuss with our partners and, in particular, with the United Nations presence on the ground, some of these issues and, where possible, to provide remedies to the satisfaction of both sides.

In conclusion, Mr. President, we want to reiterate our commitment to peaceful coexistence and cooperation with the Republic of the Sudan, as both sides stand to gain from cordial ties. I take this opportunity to reaffirm our deep appreciation for the sustained and unwavering support we have received from the international community, in particular the AU and the UN, without which we could not have done all that we have so far been able to achieve.

Thank you, Mr. President.

## 2. Statement by the Permanent Representative of the Republic of South Sudan to the United Nations, Dr. Francis Mading Deng, to the Security Council's Working Group on Children and Armed Conflict, New York, April 19, 2013

Madame Chairperson,

This being my first time to address the Working Group on Children and Armed Conflict, permit me to congratulate you on your assumption of the Chair of the Working Group and also to congratulate you on the impressive and well deserved election of your country, Luxembourg, to the Security Council. As evidenced by your election to the Chair of this Working Group, we are confident that your membership in the Security Council will be of great service not only to the Organization in general, but also to the vulnerable populations and nations in particular.

Madame Chairperson,

I have been closely associated with the issue of Children and armed conflict since I was a member of the advisory panel for the study of Madame Graça Machel, which paved the way to the creation of the mandate of the Special Representative of the Secretary-General on Children and Armed Conflict. That mandate itself was modeled after my own mandate as the Representative of the Secretary-General on Internally Displaced Persons.

Madame Chairperson,

Children present us with a striking paradox. As I have often said, they provide us all with a common ground, united in our support for their protection and general welfare. And yet, children and women are often the most victimized by conflict and related violations. In my own work on the internally displaced, I found them often the overwhelming majority in displacement camps, denied the benefits of education, health services, and physical security. As these conditions are often long lasting, the cumulative damage can be devastating to the life of a child.

Nowhere is the damage to children in armed conflict greater than the areas where the misnamed Lord's Resistance Army has inflicted unimaginable atrocities on populations generally and children in particular. As the report of the Working Group documents, these have included killing and maiming, sexual violence, abductions, recruitment, and many other forms of exploitation, not to mention general physical destruction and denial of access to humanitarian assistance.

I witnessed some of this myself when I visited Northern Uganda in my capacity as Representative of the Secretary-General on IDPs. I was informed that a lush green and most fertile region of the country, which had been known for its agricultural productivity, was rendered dormant by the activities of the LRA. Eighty-five percent of the population in the region were in displacement camps and living on international food aid. A most appalling feature was the plight of children known as night commuters, thousands of whom poured into towns at nightfall to avoid abductions by the LRA. They slept in the verandas of shops, in the hospital yards, and even in car parks. I witnessed children who had escaped or had been rescued from the LRA and who had been maimed and so traumatized that they could hardly look people in the face.

Madame Chairperson,

As the report credibly documents, the impact of LRA's terroristic activities have now assumed a regional dimension affecting no longer Uganda alone, but also the Democratic Republic of the Congo, the Republic of South Sudan and the Central African Republic. The Governments of these countries have joined hands through the regional task force to jointly fight the LRA. These Governments are also being assisted by the African Union and the United Nations. The Sudan People's Liberation Army (SPLA) of South Sudan has contributed 500 soldiers to the AU initiative. Our forces will engage positively as required by the mandate of the regional task force. As a country, we would like to see security and stability established and consolidated in our region.

Madame Chairperson,

The Report of the Working Group is laudable in both breadth and depth. It shows clearly that a great deal has been done and is still being done to combat the threat of LRA. While this is much appreciated, it is also bewildering that the LRA remains a terrorizing force over such a large territory. It will be recalled that the Government of South Sudan tried to mediate a peaceful resolution of the conflict between the Government of Uganda and the LRA. And while the process initially seemed promising, it ended in utter failure.

We welcome the Report of the Working Group as a credible documentation of what has been done and is still to be done. It must, however, be emphasized that there is still an urgent need to re-double the efforts by all concerned actors to ensure that this spreading cancer is fully eradicated within a specified period of time. Such a deadline might be a useful warning to the LRA that the end is in sight.

I thank you, Madame Chairperson, for your kind attention.


## 3. Statement Based on Talking Points for an Address to the African Group at the United Nations on the Situation in Abyei by Dr. Francis Mading Deng, Permanent Representative of the Republic of South Sudan to the United Nations, May 7, 2013

Mr. Chairman (PR of Cote d'Ivoire),

This being my first time to address the African Group since you assumed this month's chairmanship, I would like to join those who spoke before me in congratulating you and pledging the full cooperation of my delegation with you. I would also like to express our appreciation for your predecessor's (PR of the Democratic Republic of the Congo) leadership.

Mr. Chairman,

I would like to thank you most sincerely for the opportunity to address this august body on the critical developments in our area of Abyei. In the interest of time, I will focus my remarks on the events of May 4th in the area, to which you have already made reference, and their implications for the cause of peace between Sudan and South Sudan. I very much appreciate your kind words of condolence about the assassination of the Ngok Dinka Paramount Chief who, I should say, was my brother, and a very dear one. But it is not my personal relationship with him that brings me here. It is our public interest in what he represented and what his death means for the cause of peace that we all stand for.

As you noted, Mr. Chairman, on May 4th, a group of armed Missiriya intercepted a UNISFA convoy carrying the Force Commander, Major General Yohannes Tesfamariam, the Paramount Chief, Kuol Deng Kuol, Deputy Co-Chair of AJOC, Deng Mading Mijak, and other prominent Ngok personalities. They had just ended an AJOC meeting with their Sudanese counterparts who had left on their way back to Khartoum. The Paramount Chief and his Ngok Dinka companions requested UNISFA to escort them to the northern areas of Abyei, where it was alleged that there were plans by Khartoum to settle the Missiriya with the objective of changing the demographic composition of Abyei area in anticipation of the stipulated referendum in October, 2013.

The convoy was stopped by a group of armed Missiriya estimated in the hundreds. The Missiriya demanded that the Paramount Chief and the Ngok Dinka with him be handed over to them, with the expressed intention of executing them. The Force Commander of course refused to hand them over and engaged the Missiriya in negotiations that lasted about five hours, urging them to let the convoy pass, and imploring them not to harm the Paramount Chief or any of the Ngok Dinka.

When in the end the Force Commander concluded that he could not persuade the Missiriya, the convoy decided to turn around to go back to Abyei. That was the moment one of the Missiriya men shot the Paramount Chief and his UNISFA Ethiopian driver, instantly killing them.

In the ensuing exchange of fire, three more UNISFA soldiers were seriously injured and reportedly three on the Missiriya side were killed.

Mr. Chairman,

This is by no means an isolated incident, but the culmination of a trend. Reports from Abyei have demonstrated a pattern of attacks by armed Missiriya, killing people, looting cattle, and burning villages. Some of these attacks were carried out in the presence of UNISFA soldiers or were reported to them. But UNISFA invariably responded by saying that their mandate was to keep the armed forces of the Sudan and South Sudan out of the area, and not to interfere with armed civilians and their actions.

It is a well-known fact that for decades, the Government in Khartoum has been recruiting the Missiriya, training them, arming them and unleashing them, supposedly against the rebel movement in the South, but in effect turning their guns against the civilian population, primarily their immediate neighbors to the south, the Ngok Dinka. Despite all peace agreements, and the presence of UNISFA as a protection force, this pattern has continued.

When the Force Commander was in New York last month, I discussed the situation with him at length. A few days later, the Minister of Cabinet Affairs of South Sudan, Deng Alor Kuol, and the Former Co-Chair of AJOC, Dr. Luka Biong Deng, also discussed it with the Force Commander in my presence. In both meetings, he confirmed that their mandate did not authorize them to interfere with armed civilians, even though they had creatively tried to prevent Missiriya attacks.

I must note here that while the Ngok Dinka population could not understand the limitation of the mandate by a force that was ostensibly for the protection of civilians against armed groups, they also appreciated the presence of UNISFA as a major improvement on their extremely dangerous situation, having in the past been victims of unscrupulous attacks by the North in the absence or total indifference of the international community. The inadequacy of international protection is therefore a gap in what is otherwise a positive development.

The May 4th incident has the potential to generate two contrasting developments. I am a believer that in crises there may be opportunities.

We hope that the international community will be more prompted by this crisis to address the protection challenges in Abyei area by strengthening the mandate of UNISFA to protect civilians against armed elements, whether they are uniformed soldiers or armed civilians, and to re-double efforts toward the resolution of the Final Status of Abyei. Failure to address the security concerns in the area could predictably lead to the Ngok Dinka arming themselves for self-protection. This would either deter the Missiriya from attacking the Dinka or lead to the escalation of the conflict in the area and possibly trigger a return to war. Wisdom would dictate that the first option is the desirable one and that the second would be rendered unnecessary if the first was accomplished, or if both tribes were equally and credibly disarmed.

Mr. Chairman,

I would like to acknowledge, with appreciation, the calls that I have received from my Sudanese colleague, Ambassador Daffa-Alla Elhag, in which he not only expressed condolences, but also reported that the incident has shocked the people and Government of the Sudan and that it has been strongly condemned. He stated that the Government intends to conduct an investigation into the incident and hold those responsible accountable. While this pledge is to be applauded, it should be remembered that with all the massive violence and killings that Abyei has witnessed for decades, there has never been a single case of investigation, far less accountability. Judging from the history of consistent impunity in the past, the good will expressed by the Sudanese authorities would be rendered more credible if an investigation was conducted in genuine cooperation with the international community, including the African Union Peace and Security Council and the United Nations Security Council, with the participation of representatives of Sudan, South Sudan, and Ethiopia as interested parties.

The allegations of a Government programme to settle the Missiriya in the land of the Dinka in an attempt to change the demography of the area in anticipation of the stipulated referendum will also need to be investigated by an international committee. And if found to be the case, it must be immediately stopped.

Equally urgent is the need to act affirmatively in determining the Final Status of Abyei along the lines of the AU High Implementation Panel's proposal of 21st September 2012, which was endorsed by the AU Peace and Security Council, but which has so far been blocked from reaching the UNSC by the diplomatic maneuvers of Khartoum.

The slogan of "African Solutions for African Problems" is a noble one, which, of course, all Africans should support, but which needs international cooperation, specifically between the African Union and the United Nations, to be effective and internationally credible.

President Bashir's magnanimous initial response to the decision of the people of South Sudan to be independent and his declaration that the two countries would be the best of neighbors was a most welcome gesture. The two countries have witnessed for far too long the destruction and massive suffering that come with war; there is nothing to gain from war, and everything to gain from peace. But to be meaningful, peace must be truly comprehensive, as the 2005 Comprehensive Peace Agreement claims.

The progress recently reflected by the meeting of the two Presidents must be extended to Abyei. The tragedy of Abyei is that the violent conflicts of recent decades have overshadowed the positive bridging role the area has played in the history of relations between the North and the South. Paradoxically, Abyei is now the tragic victim of North-South relations that have significantly improved and look even more promising. But history has shown that Abyei can be an agent for peace or a trigger for war. Indeed, the 1983 return to war was triggered by the failure to implement the provision of the 1972 Addis Ababa Agreement that gave the area the right now given them by the CPA.

Let us not allow history to repeat itself.

## 4. Proposals for the Interim Stabilization of the Crisis Situation in Abyei, Submitted to the United Nations Security Council by the Permanent Representative of the Republic of South Sudan to the United Nations, Dr. Francis Mading Deng, May 19, 2014

I would like to begin by thanking the members of the Security Council for giving me the opportunity to share my views on an issue not only of great concern to our country of South Sudan, but also to me personally. As I am sure at least some members of the Council know, I come from Abyei. However, I hope that what I have to say is objective and constructive enough to gain the understanding and support of the Council members.

First, I would like to commend the Secretary-General for his report, which provides insightful analysis of the crisis situation in Abyei and offers constructive proposals on the way forward. I would also like to commend the UNISFA Head of Mission and Force Commander, Lieutenant-General Yohannes Tesfamariam, for his commitment and dedicated service under very trying circumstances. He has also been kind enough to keep me informed on developments in the area.

I have been in close contact with Ngok Dinka leaders, both in Juba and Abyei, including my brother Bulabek Deng, who succeeded our assassinated brother, Kuol Deng, as Paramount Chief. I met with members of the Strategic Review Team before and after their field visit. I also received from our Ministry of Foreign Affairs the ten-point recommendations which the Abyei community leaders presented to the team for strengthening UNISFA's mandate, and which have been well reflected in the Report.

The picture the Secretary-General's Report presents sadly reflects the realities on the ground as conveyed to me by these leaders. I should say that I have over the years had the opportunity to discuss the situation in Abyei with leading members of the Missiriya, Sudanese and South Sudanese leaders, and international mediators, including the Chairman of the African Union High Implementation Panel (AUHIP), former President Thabo Mbeki.

The situation now, in my opinion, has reached a point where creative ideas are needed to overcome the impasse on Abyei and to prevent the crisis from escalating into yet another catastrophic explosion in the region. The highest order of priority now is to stabilize the crisis situation in Abyei by establishing an effective administration and ensuring protection for the population to return, resettle and lead a secure and productive life without the threat of violent attacks from their neighbors.

In my opinion, the four options proposed by the Secretary-General present a critically important challenge for the United Nations and the Security Council in particular. Ending the UNISFA Mission and withdrawing the Ethiopian Forces cannot be a viable option, as it would leave a dangerous vacuum for the security of the area. Indeed, the best thing going for the population in the area is the presence of the international community through UNISFA. The recommendations of the Abyei community leaders are premised not only on the continuation of UNISFA's Mandate, but also on its being reinforced and strengthened to play a greater and more effective role for the peace, security, and development of the area.

As the Report also shows, the next two options, maintaining the status quo and UN assumption of responsibility to implement the AUHIP (Mbeki's) Proposal on Abyei, also pose significant problems. As is well known, President Salva Kiir accepted the proposal while President Bashir rejected it. We still stand in support of the proposal and would welcome further negotiations towards its implementation. The fourth option, which advocates inter-communal dialogue through the Abyei Joint Oversight Committee (AJOC) and the resumption of negotiations between the leaders of Sudan and South Sudan, is plausible, but has also confronted obstacles on both sides.

In my opinion, elements of options 2, 3, and 4 need to be combined into a hybrid proposal. UNISFA's presence, with strengthened capacity and mandate, is crucial, as is the urgent need to support Mbeki's Proposal and the equally urgent need to facilitate inter-communal dialogue to promote Ngok Dinka–Missiriya reconciliation. The combination of these elements has the potential for stabilizing the situation in Abyei and restoring cordial and cooperative relations between the Ngok Dinka and the Missiriya. The proposed four-month extension of the UNISFA Mandate, during which to develop a durable solution to the Abyei problem, is a very short period that calls for a speedy search for alternatives.

What follows are ideas which I have informally discussed with the various stakeholders over the years, including leaders on both sides, and which I now present in the hope that they may provide a common ground for all concerned during the interim or transitional period, pending agreement on the final status of Abyei. The thrust of these ideas is to establish an autonomous Abyei Area under internationally supervised security arrangements in cooperation with the Governments of South Sudan and Sudan. These arrangements would allow the area to stabilize, develop economically and restore its historic position as a bridge between Sudan and South Sudan and a hub for trading livestock, grain, and other commodities in the entire region bordering.

The proposed arrangements should provide a framework for supporting the sustainable return, resettlement, reintegration, and socioeconomic development of the Ngok Dinka population, with due consideration for, and response to, the needs of the nomadic Missiriya Humr within their area of normal residence as well as in the transitional zone of their dry seasonal migration in search of water and pasture in Abyei. It should be noted, however, that it is not only the Missiriya who migrate seasonally to the Abyei area; South Sudan's herders, both Dinka and Nuer, from several states also escape floods during the rainy season by moving to drier areas in Ngok land. This makes Abyei a genuine crossroads and bridge between Sudan and South Sudan.

In light of the security situations in both Sudan and South Sudan, the fact that they are now deadlocked over Abyei is particularly dangerous for the region. The international community urgently needs to explore ways of reconciling the conflicting positions on Abyei by addressing two interrelated concerns: those of the Ngok Dinka who, though indigenous inhabitants of the area, perceive their very survival as a people to be at risk from persistent northern invasion, and those of the neighboring Missiriya Humr who, though nomadic herders, perceive their access to seasonal water and grazing to be threatened by the prospects of Abyei joining South Sudan.

The interim or transitional measures needed to address these concerns under UNISFA can be summarized in the following points:

Consolidating support for the establishment of an autonomous administration of the Ngok Dinka, including the three organs of Government—executive, legislative, and judicial; and establishing a well-trained police force to maintain law and order;

Supporting the return and resettlement of the Ngok Dinka to their home areas in safety and dignity; and providing essential social services, particularly in the areas of health and education, and meeting the humanitarian needs of the returning and resident populations;

Facilitating the transition from humanitarian assistance to recovery and sustainable socio-economic development, including building roads, constructing upgraded housing, improving agricultural production, promoting the employment of youth and former combatants, and providing care for those made most vulnerable by war, especially women, children, and the elderly;

Identifying and meeting the immediate needs of the Missiriya and other nomadic peoples during their seasonal migration in search of water and pastures; and facilitating peace, reconciliation, and cooperative relations between the Ngok Dinka and the Missiriya Humr, as stipulated in the Abyei Protocol;

Ensuring regional and international support for these interim or transitional arrangements and their operational frameworks in cooperation with South Sudan and Sudan; soliciting financial backing from bilateral and multilateral donors, including the "TROIKA" (Norway, the United Kingdom, and the United States), the African Union, the European Union and the United Nations; and guaranteeing that the oil revenues due to the local community are made available for the provision of services and development in the area.

These points should be seen in the context of the inter-connected conflicts in the border areas of Sudan and South Sudan. Abyei can become a flashpoint that compounds conflicts in both countries or can be a model for addressing the development and governance challenges that are at the roots of these regional conflicts, especially through a system of decentralization and devolution of powers.

What I have outlined here does not substitute for the various agreements over Abyei that were negotiated with international involvement, but whose implementation is stalled. Rather, it should be seen as an interim or a transitional solution designed to promote peace, reconciliation, and cooperation among the various stakeholders and create a more conducive environment for determining the final status of Abyei.

## 5. Statement by Dr. Francis Mading Deng, Permanent Representative of the Republic of South Sudan to the United Nations, to the UN Security Council on the Situation in South Sudan and UNMISS, New York, March 18, 2014

Thank you, Madame President,

As this is the first time that my delegation addresses the Security Council during your Presidency, permit me to begin by congratulating you and your delegation on assuming the responsibility for the month of March, 2014, and wish you every success in your leadership. I would like to assure you, Madame President, of the full support and cooperation of my Delegation.

I would also like to commend your predecessor for the leadership of the Council for the month of February, when I had the honor to exchange views with her on the crisis situation in our country. I want to assure her and the Council that the concerns the Council had asked her to share with me have been duly conveyed to the authorities at home and I have been assured that they are being given serious consideration.

Permit me also Madame President to take this opportunity to thank Mr. Hervé Ladsous, Under Secretary General for the Department of Peace-Keeping Operations and take note of his statement on UNMISS operational challenges. I also thank Ms. Phumzile Mlambo-Ngcuka, Executive Director of UN Women, for her reflections on her visit to South Sudan and the current humanitarian situation. I would like to assure them both that the Government of South Sudan will give their observations due consideration and attention, with the view to improving cooperation as we jointly engage in expediting recovery for the people of South Sudan. My gratitude is also due to Ms. Hilde Johnson who has borne the burden of UNMISS responsibilities during these trying times.

Madame President,

It is of course very painful to listen to the details of the situation as have just been presented. We realize that all this is strongly motivated by desire for the colleagues in the United Nations Secretariat and, of course, the Council, to help the South Sudan people and Government. As such, and as Representative of South Sudan, my reaction cannot be one of defensiveness or denial or discomfort with hearing what has been said. All I would say, however, is that realizing that we have mutual interest in addressing the crisis and to restore peace, security and stability for our people, we need to see the situation, when possible, from both perspectives. And it is in that light that my statement will reflect my desire, our desire, to bridge the difference and to try to work together in addressing the crisis.

Despite the difficulty our relations have been confronting under the current crisis, the Government of South Sudan continues to sincerely appreciate and support the work the Security Council, the Secretary General and other bodies within the UN system continue to give South Sudan under extremely challenging circumstances.

It is to the trauma, frustrations, pain and anger caused by the devastating violence that broke out on December 15th, 2013, that much of the negative public outcry against UNMISS should be attributed. It is undeniable that had UNMISS not opened its camps to the fleeing IDPs, thousands more would have lost their lives. It is also obvious that the country has nothing to gain and much to lose by alienating the UN and the International Community at large. I know personally that the leadership of South Sudan, in particular President Salva Kiir himself, remains deeply appreciative of the role the UN is playing in the country and is unwaveringly committed to continued cooperation with the organization.

Much appreciated also is the role played by the International NGO community in collaboration with UNMISS in saving lives. We appreciate the development of the Crisis Response Plan for South Sudan which aims at continuing to save lives, as well as to help the people of South Sudan to begin the process of restoring peace and normalizing the situation in the country. As a Government, it is indeed our responsibility to do our utmost to cooperate closely with those who are trying to help us alleviate the suffering of our people.

Madame President,

The Government of South Sudan is doing its best, under very difficult circumstances, to prove to its people and indeed to the International Community that it wishes to see a speedy end to the current conflict that is devastating our country. It is well known that President Salva Kiir is strongly committed to peace, unity and national reconciliation. The Government remains committed to the IGAD talks with SPLM/A in Opposition and has agreed to the deployment of the IGAD Regional Force, as well as the Monitoring and Verification Mechanisms (MVM) in the affected areas. The SPLM/A in opposition, who currently have control of Nassir, Malakal and Akobo, have regrettably not accepted the regional force, nor the MVM.

Madame President,

In crisis, there are also opportunities. Since the process of negotiations takes time, South Sudan will probably adopt a two-phased approach. The first phase is to end the violence as soon as possible. Along with, of course, providing the much needed humanitarian assistance. The second phase will be a longer in-depth discussion of what went wrong and how the mistakes of the past can be corrected to take the nation back to the path of sustainable peace, development and prosperity that the people of South Sudan so badly need and deserve. We are deeply grateful to the regional leaders and the International Partners who have assisted South Sudan in having an opportunity to discuss differences and strategize on the way out of this crisis.

Madame President,

We cannot, of course, take lightly the anti-UNMISS sentiment that is being reflected by demonstrations across South Sudan and may indirectly have led to some SOFA infractions. I would like to assure the Security Council that this is not the policy of the Government of South Sudan. Cabinet discussions and decisions reflect the notion that the

United Nations is indeed a principal partner to South Sudan and a reflection of the good will of the international community towards our country. Again, I speak not only for the Government, but for the President personally in saying that the Government plans to exert all efforts to calm the situation down and contain hostile publicity and public display. Indeed, the Government of South Sudan deeply regrets the loss of life of Humanitarian personnel as a direct result of the heightened tensions in the conflict. I say these things, as I said, not simply as the Representative of the Government, but also as someone who has engaged with the authorities on all these issues and I note and should say, that during my visit to Juba for a Conference of the Ambassadors, I requested and was granted permission by the President to visit the detainees, both the four who were still in Juba and the seven who were in Nairobi. And I had insight into the extent to which, despite all the sharp differences, there is a profound desire among the detainees to end these hostilities as speedily as possible to restore peace, unity and reconciliation.

Despite my appreciation for all that is said by the United Nations about the Situation in our country, we appeal to the International Community to appreciate not only the democratic freedom of peaceful demonstrations, but also the frustration and anger driving the people, especially when certain actions take place which give them the impression, however mistaken, that those representing the UN may be sympathetic and supportive of the other side in the conflict. In saying so, let me emphasize, of course, that the UN cannot take sides in the conflict, but misunderstandings in a crisis situation can generate hostile reactions. As I often said, continuous engagement and constructive dialogue is a way to correct such misunderstandings. As I said, much of what I say is as a result of engaging with the leadership, the President, Vice President and relevant Ministers. In fact, earlier today, I spoke with the President and the Vice President and what I am saying is exactly what they asked me to convey to the Council.

As reflected in the Secretary General's report, the Government of the Republic of South Sudan is aware that the Security Council will be deliberating changes in the UNMISS Mandate. Given the reality of conflict in South Sudan, it is of course understandable that the Security

Council will revise its priorities and look into focusing UNMISS's mandate to the protection of civilians, human rights and security sector reform. We would, however, urge the Council to continue with some of the other crucial elements for the stabilization of the country as originally envisaged. As I have often said, South Sudan was rendered vulnerable by a war that raged for half a century and is ironically now made even more vulnerable by the current crisis. The country is more in need of international support now than it has ever been before.

Finally Madame President,

Let me conclude by reiterating our appreciation and support for the work of UNMISS and the United Nations in general, despite concerns on both sides, which I believe can be addressed and resolved through constructive dialogue.

I thank you, Madame President, for your kind attention.

## 6. Statement by the Permanent Representative of the Republic of South Sudan to the United Nations, Dr. Francis Mading Deng, to the UN Security Council on the Human Rights Situation in South Sudan, May 2, 2014

Mr. President,

As this is the first time I am addressing the Security Council under your Presidency, allow me to congratulate you and to assure you of our support and cooperation. I would also like to commend your predecessor for successfully steering the Council during the month of April.

Mr. President,

As I have previously stated to the Council, while it is painful to listen to accounts of the tragic situation in our country, our response is not to be defensive or in denial. We recognize that the motivation behind these accounts is to help South Sudan address the crisis in cooperation with the international community. That is why we have consistently expressed our sincere appreciation to the Security Council specifically, and the International Community generally, for their steadfast engagement and support.

Mr. President,

No one who believes in the ideals of human rights and in the prevention of genocide and related atrocities can quarrel with the pleas and warnings made by the High Commissioner of Human Rights and the Secretary-General's Special Advisor on the Prevention of Genocide. As I have repeatedly stated, our people struggled for decades against discrimination and gross violations of human rights. Ours was a struggle for equality and human dignity, which constitute the foundations for human rights. These principles should guide us in building our nation.

At the same time, we have consistently acknowledged that the legacy of that long war has created a culture of violence that has remained a threat to the peace and security of our people and, indeed, our nation. Responsibility for containing and transforming this persistent threat must, however, be apportioned appropriately, if we are to develop well tailored remedies.

Mr. President,

While the tendency towards moral equivalency may be understandable as a tactic and even a strategy for engaging the parties on the basis of mutual recognition and respect, it risks equating rights and wrongs in a way that clouds the situation on the ground. It is, of course, indisputable that the Government must bear the primary responsibility for protecting its citizens without discrimination on ethnic or any other ground, and be accountable in that regard. However, that cannot justify placing a democratically elected government on the same moral, political, and legal grounds with a rebel group using violence to overthrow that Government. The President told me that he had said to the High Commissioner and the Special Adviser that if they had time to spend in the country, he would encourage them to go wherever they wanted to witness developments on the ground and see who is doing what.

Nevertheless, we recognize that people do not take up arms to kill and risk being killed without some cause or grievance that should be addressed. That is why our Government, in particular President Salva Kiir, has repeatedly reaffirmed commitment to dialogue with the rebels to bring a speedy end to the violence and promote peace, unity, and national reconciliation.

Mr. President,

On specific issues raised by the reports of the High Commissioner and Advisor, the allegation that both sides are recruiting child soldiers is an example of the moral equivalency that clouds the facts and the need for targeted responsibility. It is well known that since 2003, the Sudan People's Liberation Army (SPLA) has ended recruiting or deploying child soldiers. This has indeed been acknowledged by the relevant UN bodies, which have applauded South Sudan for that action. Although the demands of the war have recently necessitated recruitment into the Army, especially with the defection of large numbers of soldiers to the rebels, it has not at all entailed recruiting child soldiers. As a prominent member of the Government told me recently, our problem is the reverse in that we have an aging army. In contrast to the Government, the rebel army is known for its recruiting and deploying child soldiers, its "White Army" being a notorious example.

On the issue of human rights violations in general, I reiterate the fact that the Government has been transparent in acknowledging the problem as part of the legacy of the war of liberation. President Salva Kiir has condemned it unequivocally and, in response to the recent developments, has created a high level committee, chaired by the former Chief Justice, to investigate gross violations of human rights and to hold accountable those found responsible. The Government has also welcomed, and pledged support for, the African Union Commission of Inquiry (COI), under the Chairmanship of former President of Nigeria, Olusegun Obasanjo, charged with investigating human rights violations resulting from the current crisis. This contrasts sharply with the situation of human rights on the part of the rebels where the massive abuses have become a conspicuous part of their war strategy, with scarcely a condemning word from the leadership.

Mr. President,

It is unfortunate that the very regrettable incident of the youth attack on the UN compound in Bor is being equated with the atrocities committed by the rebel army in Bentiu in Malakal. The Bor incident, which has been strongly condemned by the Government, was provoked by the IDPs in the UN compound celebrating the capture of Bentiu by the rebels who had only recently destroyed Bor and massacred the inhabitants. The incident was initially intended as a peaceful rally to submit a protest letter to UNMIS asking that the IDPs be removed from the area as a source of provocation, but got out of hand when the peacekeepers fired shots into the air to stop the youth from entering the camp. This was construed by the youth as an attack, provoking them to force their way into the camp. In Bentiu, the rebels had massacred hundreds of civilians, including people who had sought shelter or refuge in churches and mosques, and patients receiving care in hospitals.

Mr. President,

I would like to end my remarks with two points, which I consider crucial to a constructive response to the crisis in our country. First, we very much appreciate the concerted effort of the international community in support of the IGAD and AU peace process, and would urge continued and, indeed, elevated engagement at the highest levels to accelerate an early end to this devastating senseless violence. Second, we all recognize that after the long war in the Sudan, South Sudan has been weakened and lacks the capacity for ensuring internal peace, security, delivery of services and generating and sustaining a robust socio-economic development. These were, indeed, the reasons for the ambitious, multi-faceted support that created UNMISS. The current crisis is weakening and diminishing the limited capacity of the State even more. Although it is understandable that the UN must reconsider its priorities in light of the crisis, South Sudan needs support for capacity building now even more than it did before. Punitive measures can only compound the crisis. What South Sudan needs is understanding, compassion, and support in building a nation that can ensure peace, security, stability, and development for its people.

Mr. President,

Although our country is now acutely divided, we believe that our culture is one in which conflict can be resolved through mutual accommodation, forgiveness and reconciliation. President Salva Kiir has repeatedly stated his commitment to these values, which should provide the pillars for our peace process. In this connection, I would like to report that President Salva Kiir graciously granted me permission to meet with the four detainees in Juba and the seven who had been released and placed under the care of the Government of Kenya. All of them opposed the use of violence to overthrow the Government, but supported dialogue to address the concerns of the rebels and other opposition groups to end the war and restore peace and national reconciliation.

Mr. President,

We trust in your understanding and unwavering support for all the people of our country as the One United Nations.

I thank you.

## 7. Statement by the Permanent Representative of the Republic of South Sudan to the United Nations, Dr. Francis Mading Deng, to the UN Security Council, on the Crisis in South Sudan, New York, May 12, 2014

Mr. President,

I thank you and members of the Security Council for giving me another opportunity to address the Council on the unfolding tragic situation in our country.

The reports about the violations of human rights law and international humanitarian law associated with the devastating conflict our country has been experiencing are extremely disturbing. In my previous statement, I reported on what the Government is trying to do by creating a national investigation committee and cooperation with the African Commission of Inquiry.

On a positive note, recent developments point at a more encouraging direction towards peace.

Following the visits of the U.S. Secretary of State, John Kerry, and the UN Secretary-General, Ban Ki-moon, who successfully urged the leaders of the warring factions to meet face-to-face, President Salva Kiir and Dr. Riek Machar did meet under the mediation of the Ethiopian Prime Minister Haile Miriam Desalegn, and signed a framework agreement for a peace process.

The agreement not only stipulates immediate cessation of hostilities, in reaffirmation of the 23rd January 2014 Cessation of Hostilities Agreement, but also commits the parties to the separation of their forces and the deployment of the IGAD Monitoring and Verification Mechanism (MVM). The agreement also stipulates opening humanitarian corridors and unconditional cooperation with the UN and humanitarian agencies to ensure that humanitarian aid reaches affected populations in all areas of the country.

The Parties also agreed to establish a transitional government of national unity and engage all stakeholders, including the former detainees, political parties, civil society, and faith-based organizations to negotiate a system of transitional governance, the permanent constitution of South Sudan and any other issues concerning the future of the country, to ensure sustainable peace, unity and reconciliation.

This positive turn of events is the result of cooperation first and foremost by the leaders of South Sudan, particularly Salva Kiir Mayardit in reaching out to a rebel leader, Dr. Riek Machar, and then with the international community, specifically IGAD, the AU and the UN, further testimony to the commitment of the United Nations and the international community to support South Sudan in overcoming the formidable challenges it faces since achieving independence after half a century of devastating war with the North.

It is also a testimony to the increasing international commitment to assisting post-conflict countries in consolidating peace, security, and stability as preconditions for socio-economic development. Even more significant is the commitment to assist governments to protect their populations from the crimes of genocide, war crimes, ethnic cleansing and crimes against humanity. It is of course recognized that the primary responsibility to protect populations lies with the state, but when a state lacks the capacity to discharge that national responsibility, it is incumbent on the international community to provide the necessary support to enhance state capacity in fulfilling its national responsibility.

The case of South Sudan is one in which despite the acknowledgement of state responsibility to protect its people, the capacity of the state to do so is extremely weak due to a number of historical factors. International support to enhance capacity of the state becomes therefore critical. This is why we have argued that while the international community will need to reorder its priorities, in light of the current crisis, support for state capacity-building should remain high in the order of priorities.

We are deeply grateful to our sub-regional organization, IGAD, our continental union, the African Union (AU), the United Nations and our friends and partners in the international community for heeding our call for support.

As someone who observed the response of the United Nations firsthand as Undersecretary-General/Advisor to the Secretary-General on the prevention of genocide, I have witnessed the compassion and passion with which the Secretary-General and his senior managers have dedicated themselves to assisting South Sudan in consolidating peace, security and development. It is also known that the Troika comprising Norway, the United Kingdom and the United States, in addition to our sister countries in the region and international friends and partners, have been steadfast in their support for South Sudan before and after independence.

South Sudan has been experiencing one of the worst atrocities the world has seen in the last decades. By the same token it has also received concerted international attention and support. We hope that the spectacular accomplishment of Secretary Kerry and Secretary-General Ban Ki-moon will be sustained and will usher South Sudan to a renewed commitment to peace, security, stability and dignity for all its people.

I know that these are principles to which president Salva Kiir is deeply committed. They are also the same principles Dr. Riek Machar has invoked to justify his rebellion. This should provide a basis for a common ground. It has always been my belief that the cultural values of our people advocate peace, unity and harmony. Even when the society is shattered by violent conflict, the objective of the peace process is always to restore unity, forgiveness and reconciliation. This does not, however, mean compromising the principles of justice and accountability. The challenge then becomes how to balance these principles to maximize the positives and minimize the negatives.

We fully realize that these are the challenges our country and the international community will be facing to ensure peace while also holding accountable those responsible for gross violations of human rights and humanitarian law.

Thank you, Mr. President and distinguished members of the Council, for your kind attention.

## 8. Statement by the Permanent Representative of the Republic of South Sudan to the United Nations, Dr. Francis Mading Deng, to the UN Security Council, on the Renewal of the UNMISS Mandate, New York, May 27, 2014

Madame President,

It gives me great pleasure to address the Security Council once again during your presidency. I would like to assure you and members of the Security Council of our sincere appreciation for the renewal of the UNMISS mandate. My statement this time will be a very short message of gratitude.

There is no question that despite our shared interest in the continuation of UNMISS, we have been faced by challenges that call for constructive engagement to promote mutual understanding and cooperation. For many of us who knew the background to UNMISS presence in our country as an agent of goodwill and support, it was indeed a source of discomfort to witness anti-UN demonstrations. As I said on previous occasions, the demonstrations were due in part to misunderstandings and in part to genuine concerns about specific issues that

I discussed in depth and with candour with both sides. The demonstrations were also a reaction to the gap between the ambitious objectives of the Mission as originally articulated and the shortcomings in the delivery on the ground due to the limitations of the resources available to UNMISS. This disappointment has never detracted from the Government's appreciation of the role UNMISS and its leadership were playing in the country and our commitment to cooperation, of which President Salva Kiir assured Secretary-General Ban Ki-moon during his last visit to Juba.

Madame President,

The Security Council, the Department of Peace Keeping Operations, and the Government of South Sudan have worked closely together to resolve our differences and misunderstandings in the new configuration of UNMISS. Although our Government has had some reservations about some of the elements in the renewed mandate, we hope that with our shared concerns and better communication our cooperation will be enhanced.

Madame President,

I have repeatedly stated that the Government of South Sudan is well aware of its limitations to meet fully its commitments and aspirations for the protection of its citizens, and that the legacy of the long war stretching over half a century has left deep wounds that will take long to heal. This is why we believe that despite the understandable need for the United Nations to reconsider its priorities in light of the crisis which South Sudan is undergoing, building state capacity should remain high on the list of priorities. The objective of capacity building is to help create a state that is capable, responsible and responsive, not a state that is oppressive. Failure to help build a functioning state could lead to serious problems, which the UN and the international community might be later called upon to help address. Capacity building should therefore be seen as a form of preventative strategy. We therefore hope that it will be given serious consideration and included in the next extension of the UNMISS Mandate.

The Government of South Sudan appreciates the fact that greater attention is being placed on the protection of civilians, given the gravity of the crisis the country is going through. It is our hope, however, that there will be no more tragic crises of the kind the world has so painfully witnessed, as the parties are striving to restore peace and reconciliation, with accountability, through the IGAD-led negotiations. It is also our hope that with the refocusing of the mandate and the lessons learned from previous experience, UNMISS peacekeepers, who have at times put their own lives at risk to protect civilians, will be better prepared and equipped to respond more effectively in protecting civilians, themselves and their installations.

Madame President,

As we move forward into the future, we should modestly admit that mistakes have been committed by both sides and that we should work in close cooperation to address those past mistakes and forge an even closer partnership, in pursuing our shared objectives. South Sudan will forever be grateful for the support we received in achieving our independence and in helping build a post conflict sustainable state. We should not allow the challenges we are currently facing to undermine this solid foundation.

Thank you, Madame President and members of the Council, for your kind attention.

## 9. Statement by the Permanent Representative of the Republic of South Sudan to the United Nations, Dr. Francis Mading Deng, to the UN Security Council on the Renewal of the Mandate of the United Nations Interim Status Force for Abyei (UNISFA), New York, May 29, 2013

Mr. President,

Once again, I appreciate the opportunity to address the Security Council for the third time during your Presidency. While it is an honor and a pleasure for me to appear again before the Council, I also realize that this is sadly due to the multiplicity of crises facing our country and region. My focus today will be the situation in Abyei and how I believe we can move forward beyond the current impasse.

Mr. President,

Let me begin by welcoming the decision of the Security Council to extend the mandate of UNISFA for four months. While we believe that this is a very short period for meeting the protection challenges in the area, it provides us with an opportunity to develop more durable solutions to the Abyei problem. We must also express our profound appreciation and gratitude to the Government of the Federal Republic of Ethiopia and the Force Commander and his courageous forces for their commitment to the protection of our people. As I have often said, the best thing going for the Abyei area and the Missiriya neighbours is indeed the presence of UNISFA in the area.

Mr. President,

Permit me to express my appreciation for the very positive tone with which my fellow Sudanese colleague has spoken about the situation. This is a tone which, if acted upon in the same spirit and good will, could lead us forward. The reality however is that we have had difficulty in finding a solution moving forward. In my note, "The Interim Stabilization of the Crisis Situation in Abyei," which the Council accepted as an official document in its consideration of the resolution, I argue that the situation has now reached a point where alternative ideas are urgently needed to overcome the impasse on Abyei and to prevent the crisis from escalating into yet another catastrophic explosion in the region. In my opinion, the highest priority now must be stabilization of the situation in Abyei by establishing an effective administration and ensuring that Ngok Dinka return in safety and with dignity to their original areas of residence, resettle, and lead a secure and productive life, without the threat of violent attacks from their neighbors. Equally important is the need to address the concerns of the Missiriya, both in their own areas of normal residence and in the transitional zone of their dry season migration in search of water and pasture in the Abyei area. This requires urgent measures to promote Ngok Dinka–Missiriya dialogue toward durable peace and reconciliation.

Mr. President,

The tragedy of the Abyei situation is that recent hostilities have overshadowed at least a century of well documented peaceful coexistence and cooperation between the Ngok Dinka and the Missiriya. This exceptional cooperation was widely recognized, including by British colonial administrators, as a positive model in an environment of pervasive inter-racial, inter-ethnic, and inter-religious violence between communities along the borders of then North and South Sudan. It is indeed still being referred to as a legacy worth restoring and emulating.

The basis for these cordial ties was the recognition and respect the two communities, and especially their respective leaders, had for each other. Particularly important was the protection the Ngok Dinka leadership afforded the Missiriya and other Southern Sudanese during their seasonal migration into the area of Abyei. In this respect, it should indeed be noted that South Sudanese herders, both Dinka and Nuer, from several provinces, now states, escape floods during the rainy season by moving to the drier areas in Ngok Dinka territory. This is an important part of what makes Abyei a genuine crossroads between Sudan and South Sudan.

Mr. President,

We recognize that the international community did not approve of the Abyei Community's referendum and does not recognize the overwhelming vote in favor of joining South Sudan. It is, however widely acknowledged that the referendum was well organized, efficiently and transparently conducted and reflects the genuine aspirations of the Ngok Dinka. Yet, without the cooperation of the Sudan and the support of the regional and international organizations, expressions of such aspirations have no practical significance.

Nevertheless, it is worth recalling that the Ngok Dinka were acting in the spirit of the proposal of the African Union High Implementation Panel (AU HIP) under the chairmanship of Former President Mbeki of South Africa, that the referendum be held in October, the month the Community's referendum was indeed conducted. Furthermore, that proposal, which South Sudan accepted and Sudan rejected, was endorsed by the African Union (AU) and its Peace and Security Council (PSC) as the best way forward in addressing the challenges posed by the Abyei problem.

In October, 2013, the AU PSC indeed urged the UN Security Council to extend support to the AU HIP proposal, but the Council has not been able to respond positively to that request. In any case, it is realistic to recognize that only a negotiated settlement to which both Sudan and South Sudan will be committed in good faith will bring genuine peace, security and stability to the area. President Salva Kiir has been striving to strike a balance between supporting the aspirations of the Ngok Dinka and winning the cooperation of Sudan's President Omer El Bashir. So far, the two leaders have not been able to agree on Abyei. Meanwhile, measures are urgently needed to stabilize the security situation for both the Ngok Dinka and the Missiriya.

Mr. President,

To stabilize the situation in Abyei during the interim period, as the leaders of South Sudan and Sudan negotiate the final status of the area, it is my opinion that the Ngok Dinka need and deserve to restore their erstwhile autonomous administrative status, which was combined with cordial and cooperative relations with the Missiriya, this time under internationally guaranteed security arrangements, and in cooperation with the Governments of South Sudan and Sudan. We must remember that the Missiriya too have their own autonomous administration within Sudan's national framework. Such mutually respectful arrangements would allow the area to stabilize, develop socially and economically, and rise to the challenge of its postulated role as a bridge between the two Sudans. I should reiterate that the details of my proposals for the stabilization of Abyei are in the note I have already referred to and which is a Security Council document.

Mr. President,

The objective of my remarks is not to offer solutions for the resolution of the final status of Abyei, or to undermine the proposals under consideration, but rather to suggest ideas for normalizing the situation to promote peace, security and stability for the local population, both Ngok Dinka and the Missiriya. I also believe that this would contribute to creating a climate that is conducive to a more constructive and cooperative negotiation of the final status of Abyei by the leaders of South Sudan and Sudan. I genuinely believe that it is a win-win proposal, in sharp contrast to the current situation where both parties are losing.

Mr. President,

I would like to end with the metaphor which a Ngok Dinka elder once told me and which I have often cited. He said that Abyei is like the eye, which is so small but sees so much. I now reverse that metaphor by saying that although Abyei is so small, the eyes of the world are focused on its security and general wellbeing. I think that is a major departure from their previous suffering in isolation. I hope that this positive momentum can be sustained and that Abyei will not fall back into the abyss of past tragedies. The realization of that hope is primarily in the hands of the UN Security Council and its African partners.

I thank you, Mr. President and Distinguished Members of the Council, for your kind attention.

## 10. Statement by Dr. Francis Mading Deng, Permanent Representative of the Republic of South Sudan to the United Nations, to the UN Security Council on the Occasion of the Adoption of the UNISFA Mandate Renewal, October 14, 2014

Madame President,

As this is the first time that I address the Security Council during your presidency, allow me to express my congratulations to you and your Delegation. I assure you of my Delegation's full support as you carry this important mantle. May I also take this opportunity to acknowledge your predecessor's successful discharge of her leadership.

Madame President,

The Government of South Sudan welcomes the renewal of the UNISFA mandate that has just been adopted. I would like to take this opportunity to reiterate to the Security Council the appreciation of the people of Abyei and the Government of South Sudan for the continued support of the United Nations and the wider international community to both Sudan and South Sudan to resolve their differences on the Final Status of Abyei through peaceful means. It is, however, evident, as reflected in the Secretary General's report, that there is, regrettably, a prolonged impasse, and that new and creative ideas must be sought in order to generate the required outcome.

The Abyei Protocol of the Comprehensive Peace Agreement refers to Abyei as the area where the nine Ngok Dinka chiefdoms settled prior to the 1905 annexation of the Area to Northern Sudan. The Permanent Court of Arbitration, with the acceptance of both the Sudan and South Sudan, defined that Area, now commonly referred to as "the box." The only thing that remains to be settled is the self-determination of the Ngok Dinka, on which the people expressed themselves unequivocally in October 2013, in their Community Referendum.

Madame President,

Although the Abyei Community Referendum was well organized, efficiently and transparently conducted, and resulted in a 99.8% vote in favour of joining South Sudan, that vote has not been recognized by the International Community. As you know, Madame President, a high level team from Juba, comprised of the Chairman of the Abyei High Committee on the Referendum and two senior Ambassadors, now in New York, and who I believe are seated right behind me, have agreed to advocate for the recognition of the results of the Abyei Community Referendum. While we hope that their efforts will bear fruits, we realize that such recognition will not be forthcoming.

It should, however, be recalled that the African Peace and Security Council at its 405th meeting on November 16, 2013, reaffirmed its communiqué of October 26, 2013, which among other things reiterated its full acceptance of the AUHIP proposal on Abyei and renewed its appeal to the United Nations Security Council to urgently support the proposal as the best way forward for the solution of Abyei. If the results of the Abyei Community Referendum are not recognized, at least the proposals of the AUHIP should be pursued and implemented toward an internationally conducted and recognized referendum. Failure to act on these two grounds poses a tragic situation for the people of Abyei.

We are most appreciative of the Secretary-General's observation that "the people of Abyei Communities remain bereft of basic social services and vulnerable to ethnic based violence. The status quo cannot continue." Along those lines, we strongly support the results of the recently conducted strategic review of UNISFA aimed at developing "proposals for operational support . . . in particular as they pertain to the stabilization of Abyei."

Madame President,

An important factor in the stabilization process is inter-communal dialogue, which, as the Secretary General's report notes, hinges on a number of issues. Foremost among them is the urgency for the two communities "to find closure to the issue of the assassination of the Ngok Dinka Paramount Chief." A step in that direction should be the release of the report of the AU Investigation Committee into the assassination of the Chief and holding those accountable. There is also need to address the dispute stemming from cattle rustling. We welcome the Secretary-General's "appeal to both countries' leaders to ensure that a formal inter-communal conference commence as soon as possible," provided that a conducive climate is created.

In that context, it must be noted that, in addition to a closure on the assassination of the Paramount Chief, the issue of armed Sudan Oil Police in Diffra-Kech, which is in violation of the 20 June 2011 Agreement and the relevant UN resolutions, must be resolved. The report of the Secretary-General states that UNISFA also observed the presence of small numbers of Sudan People's Liberation Army (SPLA) personnel in Southern Abyei, in contravention of the Agreement and Security Council resolutions. One way of addressing this tendency toward moral equivalency is to send an investigation committee to verify the facts on the ground.

Madame President,

The Government of South Sudan welcomes the decision of the Secretary-General to appoint a Civilian Head of Mission to aid in the pursuance of targeted and effective humanitarian intervention to address the dire needs of the Ngok Dinka and facilitate their recovery and cooperation with the Missiriya nomads. Such peaceful interaction and cooperation between the two communities would encourage Sudanese and South Sudanese to find acceptable and creative solutions on the resolution of the Final Status of Abyei. In this connection, both countries will need the support of the AU and the UN in addressing the security, political, humanitarian and development challenges in Abyei and for both the Ngok Dinka and the Missiriya nomads.

Finally Madame President,

I would like to reiterate my Government's profound appreciation for the support already being provided by the International community, particularly the Government of Ethiopia through its invaluable contributions to UNISFA, a crucial force for the security of the Ngok Dinka and other communities that come to the area.

I thank you for your kind attention.

## 11. Statement by the Permanent Representative of the Republic of South Sudan to the United Nations, Dr. Francis Mading Deng, to the UN Security Council on the Renewal of the UNMISS Mandate, New York, November 25, 2014

Mr. President,

Let me begin by congratulating you for the assumption of the Presidency of the Council for the month of November, and assure you of my delegation's support and cooperation during your tenure. We welcome the Council's renewal of the UNMISS mandate and would like to express our profound appreciation to the troops and police contributing countries for their enormous contribution to the peacekeeping force, despite the unfavorable conditions under which they operate. Allow me also to express my gratitude to the United Nations Secretary-General, H. E. Mr. Ban Ki-moon, for his most recent report on South Sudan, and his constructive engagement with developments in our country.

Mr. President,

The current conflict in the Republic of South Sudan can only be resolved by the people of South Sudan, albeit with the assistance of the international community. As stated by the Secretary-General, "the primary responsibility for resolving the problems of South Sudan rests squarely with its leaders. The international community can support these efforts, but cannot deliver a solution from outside." It is from this premise that the Government has sincerely committed itself to the peace process with the SPLM in Opposition since the outbreak of violence in December 2013. Despite repeated cease fire violations and retaliations, the Government remains optimistic that an amicable peace agreement is possible and indeed imperative.

Mr. President,

The frustration of the international Community with the pace of talks in Addis Ababa is understandable, but a sustainable solution to the current crisis in South Sudan cannot be achieved by the imposition of sanctions, which is now being talked about and is alluded to in the report. It is a well-known fact that sanctions hardly ever achieve their intended objective. Instead, they only tend to harden positions toward confrontation rather than cooperation. We believe that the international community can play a positive role by engaging both parties constructively to expedite concluding an agreement, as was the case with the Comprehensive Peace Agreement of 2005, which brought an end to the long civil war in the Sudan.

As President Kiir has noted, the slow pace of the talks is, at least in part, attributable to the frequent adjournments of the talks by the IGAD mediators. In fact, the present adjournment is said to be giving the opposition rebel commanders the opportunity to sort out their differences.

Mr. President,

On the humanitarian front, the situation in the war-affected areas remains grave. The Government is thankful that a catastrophic famine appears to have been averted. This is largely due to the steadfast efforts of our international partners, non-governmental organizations and the friends of South Sudan. We are most grateful to them all.

Mr. President,

The situation of the IDPs in the UN camps across the country remains of great concern. The current report documents incidents of violence in the UNMISS camps which are perpetrated against other IDPs, humanitarians and UNMISS personnel, caused by unruly youth under the influence of substances. It is our sincere belief that the UNMISS camps should only be temporary arrangements or a transition to durable solutions. They cannot be an alternative to addressing the root causes of internal displacement and finding durable solutions. We hope that the on-going discussions and consultations between the Inspector General of Police and humanitarian partners, as well as with the community leaders in the protection sites, aimed at improving the security environment in selected neighborhoods in Juba to facilitate voluntary returns of IDPs, will soon bear fruits.

Mr. President,

The reported incidents of rampant human rights and humanitarian violations, including rapes and other acts of sexual violence, allegedly committed by the SPLA, confront us with a dilemma. On the one hand, as I have often stated, we do not want to be in denial or to appear to condone such outrageous criminal violations. On the other hand, many of the incidents in the report appear to be just allegations. As in most cases, allegations of such repulsive behavior are likely to provoke defensiveness. It is therefore important that such allegations be substantiated so that the perpetrators can be apprehended and brought to justice.

The Government is genuinely intolerant of these alleged practices, which are a gross violation of our own cultural values. This is evident in the fact that during the visit of the SRSG on Sexual Violence to South Sudan in October, 2014, the President signed with her a joint communiqué on addressing conflict-related sexual violence. As explained in the report, this agreement contains a set of practical and political commitments to end the use of sexual violence in conflict and provides for the creation of an action plan for the SPLA and national police. Its main objective is to ensure proper investigation of sexual violence crimes; the establishment of accountability mechanisms; the exclusion of perpetrators of sexual violence from amnesty provisions; and the explicit addressing of sexual violence in the peace process, as well as in the monitoring and implementation of cessation of hostilities agreement.

Mr. President,

The Government has taken serious steps in addressing the issue of recruitment of children into the army or their use for military purposes. The Ministry of Defense and Veteran Affairs, in collaboration with the Ministry of Justice, made constructive proposals and amendments to the SPLA Act of 2009. The amendments which became part of the new SPLA Act set out punitive measures against SPLA officials who recruit children or use schools for military purposes and commit other violations against children. Furthermore, the Government has been working closely with UNMISS in launching different initiatives and campaigns aimed at bringing to an end the recruitment and military use of children by 2016.

Mr. President,

The removal of capacity building from the UNMISS mandate has impacted negatively on the vitally important area of developing the capacity of a new and weak state, especially in the area of law enforcement agencies and institutions. As indicated by the Secretary-General's report, "the lack of any meaningful judicial system continues to impact due process protections" in South Sudan. In light of the weakness of institutions in South Sudan, which affects the government's capacity to provide essential services in conformity with international standards, it would be advisable for the Council to re-consider and re-instate this crucial element of the UNMISS mandate. We also join the Secretary-General in urging international partners and donors to double their efforts towards meeting humanitarian funding shortfall.

In conclusion, we once again reiterate our appreciation for the extension of UNMIS mandate for another 6 months and remain committed to close cooperation with the Mission.

Thank you, Mr. President, for your kind attention.

## 12. Statement by the Permanent Representative of the Republic of South Sudan to the United Nations, Dr. Francis Mading Deng, to the UN Security Council on the Adoption of the Presidential Statement by the Security Council on sanctions regime for South Sudan, March 24, 2015

Mr. President,

I am pleased and honoured to address the Council under your stewardship concerning the Presidential Statement on South Sudan.

Mr. President,

We have spoken on this issue on so many occasions that there is no longer much to be said. We have always acknowledged that the measures taken by the Security Council emanate from its deep concern about our country and people and their suffering under the current crisis. However, we believe this can be better done through constructive engagement and not through threats of punitive action. It is also a source of concern for our delegation that the Council continues to deliberate on important issues of peace and security in South Sudan without adequate consultations with the African region. This is not in line with the spirit of the Cooperation Framework between the African Union Peace and Security Council and the United Nations Security Council. Equally, although my delegation is sometimes courteously consulted on the UNSC draft resolutions or statements pertaining to South Sudan, a gesture we sincerely appreciate, our views are hardly ever reflected in the Council's final documents.

Mr. President,

The Government of the Republic of South Sudan is committed to the peaceful solution of the conflict in our country. President Salva Kiir has emphatically made the point on numerous occasions, including in his most recent statement to the nation last Wednesday, March 18, 2015. In this respect, we commend the Intergovernmental Authority for Development (IGAD) for its relentless efforts in searching for a peaceful settlement of the crisis in South Sudan.

Indeed, my Government has been engaged in the peace talks in good faith and has accepted various proposals tabled by the mediators in all rounds of the talks, including the establishment of a Transitional Government of National Unity (TGoNU). Due to his desire for inclusivity in IGAD peace talks, the President of the Republic allowed for the participation of a wide range of stake-holders, including faith-based groups, civil society organizations, youth, women and political parties to ensure national ownership of the peace process.

Mr. President,

In contrast to the good will attitude of the Government in negotiating, the SPLM-IO under the leadership of Dr. Riek Machar continues to shift positions and put forth unreasonable demands on the table, which has made it extremely difficult to reach consensus on contentious national issues. In the last round of talks, the rebels demanded two armies during the 30-month interim period, followed by amalgamation rather than integration of forces, as should be the case. They also demanded the position of 1st Vice President and 50/50 share in the formation of the government. It is incomprehensible that a country can have two separate armies under two different commands. Instead, the Government proposed the integration of rebel forces into the national army, a practice that has been successfully tested in countries emerging from civil wars across the globe and particularly in Africa.

The SPLM-IO also demanded that the Government should pay the debt incurred during their rebellion, introducing a new formula for wealth sharing. In other words they are asking the Government to pay them for the weapons and ammunition which they acquired and used to support their rebellion and kill innocent civilians in South Sudan. Again the Government did not see any justification for these demands, except that they were meant to create obstacles in reaching an agreement within the time frame of 5th March, given by IGAD. Therefore, the moral equivalency reflected in the Council's presidential statement, which expresses disappointment that both President Salva Kiir and Dr. Riek Machar have failed to conclude an agreement on the transitional arrangements as was outlined in the 1 February, 2015 is regrettably misleading.

Mr. President,

President Salva Kiir in his recent public address to the people of South Sudan extended an olive branch of peace to the SPLM-IO and Former Detainees. The President called upon the SPLM-IO to accept the general amnesty he offered and return to their units, with their previous SPLA ranks. And he ordered the Chief of General Staff to send directives to all SPLA units to receive the rebels and to provide them with necessary assistance. Furthermore, the President called upon the Former Detainees to come home and contribute toward implementing the SPLM reunification agreement, which was signed on 21st January, 2015, in Arusha, Tanzania.

Mr. President,

As I have stated to the Council on different occasions, I strongly believe that sanctions rarely achieve their intended objectives, but only encourage the hardening of positions towards confrontation. The international community can use more constructive and productive means of engaging the parties than sanctions. The Government is deeply concerned about the plan to impose sanctions, rather than adopt measures that will encourage the parties to cooperate with the international community for peace. Sanctions at this critical juncture in the history of South Sudan will only devastate the economy, increase economic pressures and inflict additional hardship on a people who are already suffering and desperate.

Mr. President,

Despite our differences we are sincerely appreciative of the positive motives behind the Council's measures and of the opportunity granted us to share our views. We remain hopeful that in this exchange of views a common ground can emerge, divisive measures can be avoided, and productive actions can be agreed upon.

Thank you, Mr. President and distinguished members of the Council, for your kind attention.

## 13. Statement by the Permanent Representative of the Republic of South Sudan to the United Nations, Dr. Francis Mading Deng, to the UN Security Council on the Occasion of the Briefing and Consultations on the Mandate of UNMISS, May 14, 2015

Madam President,

Thank you for giving me the opportunity once again to address the Council on this issue of great significance to my country.

This being my first time to address this Council under your presidency, allow me to congratulate you for the assumption of the leadership of the Council for the month of May and to pledge our support and cooperation with you and your team. I would also like to commend your predecessor for successfully leading the Council during the month of April.

I also want to express our appreciation for the work of the Secretary-General's Special Representative in South Sudan, whose commitment, dedication and cooperative approach have gained her wide admiration in the country and internationally. We have also listened with obvious interest to the statement of the Chairman of the Sanctions Committee on the progress of their work. We pledge our cooperation with the Chairman, his Committee and the panel of experts.

Madam President,

The frequency with which I address the Council is, needless to say, due to the grave crisis situation in my country. It is an honour I wish I did not need. It is also a situation which confronts us with a dilemma. On the one hand, as I have often said, although we do not always agree, we realize that the Council's sustained occupation with our country's situation stems from the concern of the international community with the tragic conflict in the country and its dire humanitarian consequences, for which we are sincerely grateful. On the other hand, it raises many issues on which we have genuine differences of opinion.

Madam President,

There can be no doubt about our common interest in restoring peace, security and stability in our country. We are all aggrieved by the death and suffering of our innocent people. Our differences therefore do not lie in the overriding goal of peace, and the need to protect civilians, but in the methods of achieving them. For instance, the many allegations of gross violations of human rights and humanitarian law can be debated and in any situation where these allegations are made, as there are different perspectives and therefore controversies. On the other hand, it has been our principle not to be in denial or to be defensive about allegations of human rights violations. As people who believe in the ideals of human rights, we have a common interest in fighting violations of human rights, while at the same time, the details can create different perspectives on what actually happens on the ground.

On the issue of sanctions and other punitive measures, if they were sure to facilitate and accelerate the achievement of peace, there would be no controversy over them. Our position has been that rather than promote peace, they are likely to harden positions and generate confrontation. This would undermine the needed cooperation in the peace process. We believe that the international community, both as a collectivity and as concerned individual members, have the moral authority and the leverage to exert pressure by engaging the parties constructively, rather than by antagonizing them through threats of punitive actions.

We also believe that the efforts of the Government, in particular President Salva Kiir for the cause of peace, are not being adequately recognized and rewarded. For a democratically elected leader confronted with a rebellion aimed at overthrowing him, to have moved so fast from the outbreak of the rebellion, to engage his adversaries in a dialogue for peace, and to make the major compromises President Kiir has made, is remarkable. Granting amnesty to those waging war against the state, inviting them to return and join the political process, even restoring them to their former positions in the leadership, not to mention agreeing to form a transitional government of national unity and to share power with them, might strike some people as encouraging impunity, but they indicate a serious commitment to the quest for peace.

We acknowledge that pursuing peace requires engaging the warring parties with a degree of objectivity, impartiality and parity. But rights and wrongs, although never one sided, are also never equal. The risk with moral equivalency is that the wrongdoer is equated with the wronged, and that cannot be a basis for finding a truly just solution.

Madam President,

We remain deeply appreciative of the IGAD mediation efforts. Indeed, the speed with which these efforts were undertaken soon after the outbreak of hostilities in December 2013 was quite impressive. Since then, IGAD's efforts have received sustained support from the AU, the UN, in particular UNMISS, and a wide array of other international partners. However, the reports of the Secretary-General, his Special Representative, and other UN bodies indicate that the challenge is formidable and calls for a re-doubling of efforts. It is very painful to read the details of pervasive violence in the country, especially in the three most affected states, and while some may see the glass half-empty and others half-full, restoring peace must be a top priority for the parties and international partners.

Madam President,

As I see it, history is about to repeat itself. The IGAD initiative in the early 1990s that eventually culminated in the 2005 Comprehensive Peace Agreement (CPA) began with a very promising Declaration of Principles (DOP). With time, the process began to stall as regional partners began to differ among themselves. The process was then reinforced and reinvigorated by the Friends of IGAD who evolved into an IGAD Partners Forum, with the Troika of Norway, UK and US playing a leading and ultimately successful role.

It is now widely acknowledged that the IGAD mediation process is being severely challenged and is showing signs of exhaustion. It needs to be reinforced and reinvigorated. The fact that the principle of IGAD+5 is being seriously considered is an encouraging sign. But it needs to be acted upon and even more needs to be done, and urgently.

Madam President,

We are also encouraged by what appears to be an increasing willingness to offer more capacity building support in some critical areas in the new order of priorities for UNMISS, especially in the security sector. We have always said that while it is understandable that the UN needed to reorder its priorities in light of the current situation of conflict, capacity building need not be viewed as a means of empowering the Government to be more repressive or oppressive, but should be seen as a way of developing more responsible and responsive institutions of good governance, capable of protecting the civilian population and ensuring their general welfare. We have been receiving very positive reports about the cooperation of the leadership of the Police Force with UNMISS and we welcome the prospects for increased collaboration to enhance the protection role of the security forces, particularly the police.

Related to police services is the prison system, which desperately needs reform. Equally important is the judicial system and the qualification of the judges, especially in light of the call for accountability. These are some of the priority areas that call for capacity building and support from the UN.

Finally, Madam President, while the sanctions regime now appears to be in place and about to be operationalized, we still strongly advocate constructive engagement between the international community and the parties, in particular the Government. A great deal can be done through positive collaboration, while confrontation carries risks that can be counter-productive. Although war cannot be ended overnight by the actions of one side, I trust that an agreement on specific actions that the Government could take, with clear benchmarks, could encourage cooperation with the international community. A great deal of international good will has already been invested in South Sudan. It would be tragic if that were to dissipate and deny the people of South Sudan, who have already suffered from decades of devastation, the protection, assistance and development support they so desperately need.

Thank you, Madam President and Distinguished Members of the Council, for your kind attention.

# 14. Statement by Dr. Francis Mading Deng, Permanent Representative of the Republic of South Sudan to the United Nations, to the United Nations Security Council (UNSC) on the Renewal of the United Nations Interim Security Force in Abyei (UNISFA) Mandate

Mr. President,

Since this is the first time for me to speak to the Council under your Presidency, I would like to congratulate you for the leadership of the Council this month and pledge our full cooperation. I would also like to acknowledge the role of your predecessor in leading the Council last month.

Mr. President,

I have addressed the Council on this issue on so many occasions that there is not much more to be said other than reiterate some important points. I would like to welcome the renewal of the UNISFA Mandate and its extension to 15 December 2015.

Mr. President,

As I have said on numerous occasions, UNISFA is the best thing that has happened to Abyei Area for decades. Without international protection and assistance, the Ngok Dinka have always been victims of unrestrained attacks from their Northern neighbors, supported by successive governments of Sudan. Despite blatant atrocities, no one has ever been held accountable. Although UNISFA by no means provides full protection, at least the threat of uncontrolled and unaccountable attacks from the North has been reduced. I know that whenever attacks take place and the Ngok Dinka fall victim, such as the well-known case of the assassination of the Paramount Chief under the protective escort of UNISFA, the Ngok Dinka understandably see more of the negative than the big picture of protection. It should be remembered that before UNISFA was deployed, Abyei was massively invaded in 2008 and then again in 2011 by the forces of the Sudan government, that forced the civilian population to flee. This had the effect of depopulating the area.

Most of the civilian population has not yet been able to return out of fear of further attacks from the North.

Despite the shortcoming of the protection role of UNISFA, it is the only source of protection for the Ngok Dinka. In view of the fact that the impasse on the final status of Abyei between Sudan and South Sudan has now become a deadlock, and considering that the present arrangement under UNISFA cannot continue indefinitely, the Security Council is called upon to find a workable solution that will be acceptable to both sides in the conflict.

Mr. President,

I believe that some refinement of the present arrangements under UNISFA that would turn the area into an international protectorate to ensure security, provide services and generate socioeconomic development is the most practical way forward. The issue of a final status of Abyei can then be negotiated within a reasonable timeframe and in an atmosphere of relative cooperation between the two Governments reinforced by the constructive engagement of the international community.

Mr. President,

Reading the report of the Secretary-General, I believe considerable progress in providing protection and assistance has been made. But the challenge of security, stability, and development for the area remains formidable. In this context, I would like to reiterate what I have said on a number of occasions, that the nine chiefdoms of Abyei have always been administered autonomously. What is called for now is, just as the Missiriya are self-administering within their area of normal residence, the Ngok Dinka need to have all organs of Government—legislative, executive, and judiciary—under their autonomous control.

An institution of cooperation between the Ngok Dinka and Missiriya, whether through a committee or a council or through AJOC, can then manage bi-lateral relations and resolve conflicts between them. Any idea about a joint administration, whereby the Missiriya, while fully self-governing, participate in the administration of Ngok Dinka area, would be unacceptable by normative standards and would be rejected by the Ngok Dinka and the Government of South Sudan.

In addition to the security imperatives of the area, the people of Abyei are in desperate need of services, infrastructure, and socio-economic development. This can be done in partnership with UN agencies, inter-governmental organizations, non-governmental organizations, and local community-based structures, along the continuum from humanitarian assistance to relief, recovery, and development. Without these essentials, it is unlikely that the people of Abyei will return to their normal areas of residence and would remain refugees and internally displaced persons indefinitely. The Ngok Dinka of Abyei are currently virtually stateless and so their displacement remains a source of instability for the region.

In developing a solution for the area, I would hope the Security Council, in collaboration with the African Union, would find these suggestions useful in formulating a program of interim stabilization of the Abyei situation.

Finally Mr. President,

The Ngok Dinka and the Missiriya have lived as friendly and co-operative neighbors under their respective leadership for centuries. What is needed now is to restore those erstwhile cordial ties between the two communities and to turn the adversarial penetration of national authorities into promoting cooperation between the two communities.

Thank you for your attention.

FRANCIS MADING DENG is the first Permanent Representative of the newly independent country of South Sudan to the United Nations. Before assuming this position, he was the Special Adviser of the UN Secretary-General on the Prevention of Genocide at the level of Under-Secretary-General. He has also served as Representative of the Secretary-General on Internally Displaced Persons, as Sudan's ambassador to the Nordic Countries, Canada, and the United States, and as Minister of State for Foreign Affairs of Sudan. Dr. Deng is one of the directors of CIHC who also serves on the advisory board of IIHA.

DANIEL JOK M. DENG is a Senior Advisor to the Japan International Cooperation Agency (JICA) in South Sudan. He has also served as Advisor to local government and ministries in South Sudan. He has worked for international NGOs, UN agencies, inter-governmental organizations, and the private sector in the Democratic Republic of Congo (DRC), Zimbabwe, South Africa, and South Sudan.

KEVIN M. CAHILL, M.D., is University Professor and Director of Fordham University's Institute of International Humanitarian Affairs and President of The Center for International Humanitarian Cooperation in New York City. He has also served as Chief Adviser for Humanitarian and Public Health issues for successive Presidents of the United Nations General Assembly.

The CIHC is a U.S. registered public charity that was founded by, among others, former U.S. Secretary of State Cyrus Vance and John Cardinal O'Connor (both now deceased) in 1992 to promote healing and peace in countries shattered by natural disasters, armed conflicts, and ethnic violence. The Center employs its resources and unique personal contacts to stimulate interest in humanitarian issues and to promote innovative educational programs and training models. Our extensive list of publications and regular symposia address both the basic issues and the emerging challenges of humanitarian assistance. Since 2001, the CIHC has supported training in humanitarian activities through the Institute of International Humanitarian Affairs (IIHA) at Fordham University; it has now educated over 2,500 humanitarian aid professionals from 133 nations, and continues to offer programs in Europe, Asia, Africa, Latin America, and North America. The CIHC has formal partnerships with the Royal College of Surgeons in Ireland, University College Dublin, the NOHA network of European universities, United Nations World Food Programme (WFP), International Organization of Migration (IOM), International Medical Corps (IMC), Action Contre la Faim (ACF), Jesuit Refugee Service (JRS), the British Ministry of Defense, and other UN, NGO, and governmental organizations. The Directors of the CIHC serve as the Advisory Board of the IIHA. The President of the CIHC, Kevin M. Cahill, M.D., is University Professor and Director of the

Institute and Director of the Exhibition and Study Center for the History of Medicine at Lenox Hill Hospital. The CIHC Humanitarian Programs Director is Visiting Professor at the IIHA; and other CIHC Directors are Diplomats-in-Residence at Fordham University. For more information, please refer to our website: www.cihc.org.

## ABOUT THE IIHA

The Institute of International Humanitarian Affairs (IIHA) was created at Fordham University in December 2001 to forge partnerships with relief organizations, offer rigorous academic and training courses at the graduate and undergraduate level, host symposia, and publish books relating to humanitarian affairs.

The IIHA enables humanitarian workers to develop relationships with the University and the international community in New York City, in addition to being a university wide center reporting directly to the President of Fordham. With the creation of a graduate Masters and under-graduate Minor and Major degree programs, the IIHA offers an academic base for the study and development of international health, human rights, and other humanitarian issues, especially those that occur in periods of conflict.

Through multi-disciplinary coursework in humanitarian assistance, negotiations, and disaster management, the IIHA equips students with the tools needed to respond thoughtfully and effectively in humanitarian crises. The IIHA combines the theoretical and practical aspects of humanitarian affairs to generate debate, initiate discourse, and encourage information sharing among participants and faculty.